"Certainly the most thorough and extensive treatise on the theory and practice of bicycle gearing I've ever encountered."
— Steve Ready, Director
Interbike

"This book is a good information source for gearing — so far the best I have seen. It explains everything in a way that can be understood, the way I would explain gearing when I was managing a bicycle shop, and the way I explain gearing to participants in our trips. It can help you enjoy bicycling more and improve your cycling skills, whether you are just getting started in bicycling or have been cycling for years."
— Don Lange, Trips/Leadership Director
BikeCentennial

"Use your bicycle to its full advantage! Cyclists of all skills will benefit from this valuable information, presented in a thorough but readily understandable manner."
— John H. Cornelison, Executive Director
League of American Wheelmen

Bicycle Gearing

A PRACTICAL GUIDE

Dick Marr

The
Mountaineers
Seattle

To: My Father

The Mountaineers: Organized 1906 " . . . to explore, study, preserve, and enjoy the natural beauty of the Northwest."

3 2
5 4 3 2

Published by The Mountaineers
1011 S.W. Klickitat Way, Suite 107, Seattle, WA 98134

Published simultaneously in Canada by Douglas & McIntyre, Ltd., 1615 Venables Street, Vancouver, B.C. V5L 2H1

Published simultaneously in Great Britain by Cordee, 3a DeMontfort Street, Leicester, England LE1 7HD

Manufactured in the United States of America

Illustrations by Rich Weber
Cover design by Nick Gregoric
Book design by Nick Gregoric

Library of Congress Cataloging-in-Publication Data

Marr, Dick, 1938—
    Bicycle gearing : a practical guide / by Dick Marr.
        p.   cm.
    Bibliography: p.
    Includes index.
    ISBN 0-89886-184-5 :
    1. Cycling.   2. Gearing.   I. Title.
GV1043.7.M3   1989
796.6—dc19

89-2986
CIP

CONTENTS

Part II   Selecting a New Gearing

Appendices

TO READERS WITH MATH ANXIETY

Can you count from 1 to 54? Certainly you can.

When you look at three numbers like 59, 64, and 70, do you recognize that 59 is the smallest and that 70 is the largest? Of course you do.

Then you know enough mathematics to learn to use the gears on your bicycle, and to increase your riding pleasure immensely!

Don't let the many numbers found in this book prevent you from enjoying your bicycle to the fullest extent possible. Learning to use your two shift levers is easy!

PREFACE

The primary purpose of this book is to show the millions of multi-speed bicycle owners how to use their two shift levers properly, and how to increase their bicycling pleasure in the process. No other book adequately explains this topic. The thousands of riders who know that proper shifting is easy to learn have acquired the necessary information by word-of-mouth, or from magazine articles now out of print. This book provides a permanent source from which anyone who rides any type of bicycle, whether with a friction or an indexed shifting system, can easily learn to shift gears properly.

The second purpose of this book is to provide information needed to select a new gearing. Many riders significantly increase their enjoyment by personally selecting gearings which fit their needs. The extensive appendices provide many gearings from which to choose and include gearings suitable for general recreational riding, street riding, commuting, off-pavement mountain bike use, and touring. Gearings for racing are not included, although beginning racers may find some sections of this book helpful.

ACKNOWLEDGMENTS

Whenever I take an extended bicycle trip the "country folk" met along the way seem more friendly than the "city folk" back home. But as I think of all the suburbanites who have helped with the preparation of this book, I am forced to conclude that both groups are equally friendly. Perhaps the more relaxed style of country living just creates an illusion of a higher degree of friendliness.

Especially helpful with this project were Jacki and Mike Curry, Bill Davis, Bob Schreiner (of Bob's Bike Shop, in Park Ridge, IL), Mary Ellen and Dick Spirek (of Bikes Plus, Ltd., in Arlington Heights, IL), Bill Turner, and Marilyn Wilkerson. The book would not have been the same without their excellent comments, suggestions, knowledge, and advice.

Others who contributed in important ways are Jim Andresen (of ABC Cyclery, in Arlington Heights, IL), Frank Berto, Lee Borowski, Dean Folkes, Keith Kingbay, Bob Koch, Irene and George Krueger, Jeff Lovell, Marilyn and George Mathison, Dave Maurer, Stanley Natanek, Mike Nisen, Joan Parojic, Bob Ranieri, Rick Spirek, Molly Warren, Rich Weber, Andy Wilson, and Debbie and Norma Witherbee.

The Mountaineers are to be commended for their policy of providing assistance to outdoor enthusiasts who, like myself, are not professional authors. Editorial Manager Steve Whitney and Editor Rick May deserve the credit, and thanks, for skillfully and tactfully turning my "raw" manuscript into a highly respectable book. Also to be thanked are Donna DeShazo, Marge Mueller, and the bicycling members (whose names are unknown to me) of the Editorial Review Committee who recognized the need for this type of book in the bicycling world.

Finally I would like to take this opportunity to express my appreciation to all members of the Arlington Heights Bicycle Association, the Mount Prospect Bike Club, and the Wheeling Wheelmen, not only for their direct and indirect influence on this book, but also for the pleasure they have added to my life.

INTRODUCTION

The main reason that bicycle gearing remains a mystery to so many eager riders is that there is no indicator on the bicycle that identifies the gears and shows how to position the two shift levers in order to get the bicycle into each gear. With 10, 12, 14, 15, 18, or 21 ways to arrange the two levers, it is no wonder that many people do not use their gears effectively. Even automobiles, which have only one shift lever, are equipped with such a diagram or indicator.

With the aid of this book, it's easy to make a gearing chart to tape to your bike's frame or handlebars. This small chart identifies the gears that are on your bicycle, and will help you shift easily and effectively.

Part I (Chapters 1–5) discusses the effective use of the gears that are presently on your bicycle. Chapter 1 explains the need for gears and the pleasures to be derived from properly operating a modern-day bicycle. Chapter 2 explains the terminology needed to understand the other chapters by carefully identifying, with appropriate diagrams, the five parts of the bicycle that produce the gears. Chapter 3 contains the step-by-step procedure for producing the table that identifies which gears are on your bicycle and their chain positions. Chapter 4 provides necessary information about actual shifting and suggests a beginning strategy of shifting.

Chapter 5 discusses how to develop a personal pre-determined plan (strategy) of shifting; anyone who bicycles regularly can benefit by having such a plan. Experienced riders have their own strategies and always know what their next upward or downward shifts are likely to be. Strategies appropriate for 10-, 12-, 15-, and 18-speed bicycles are discussed.

Part II (Chapters 6–8) is concerned with selecting a new gearing for your bicycle. Chapter 6 explains how the gearing components relate to one another, their limitations, and other facts needed when considering a gearing change. This enables you to choose appropriately from the components available from a dealer or catalog. (Working with tools to change components is not included as this information may be found in many excellent bicycle repair manuals.)

Chapter 7 describes the advantages and disadvantages of the different types of gearings (Half-step, Alpine, Wide-step, and Crossover) frequently chosen by bicyclists, and the shifting strategies used with them. Chapter 8 discusses how to select a gearing that fits your personal needs. The extensive appendices provide enough gearings to enable you to find either the exact gearing you want or one sufficiently close to your requirements to require only slight modification.

PART I

USING YOUR GEARS EFFECTIVELY

1. WHY SO MANY GEARS?

PRELIMINARY REMARKS

The first rule of this book is that *bicycle riding is supposed to be fun!* The presence of gears adds to your fun — provided you know how to use them. And that is what this book is about: how to use the gears on *any* multi-speed bicycle that has two shift levers.

Consider the following scenario.

Two bicyclists are happily pedaling along on their multi-speed bicycles when, because of a hill or a change in the wind, the pedaling becomes difficult. It is time for them to shift gears and return to easier pedaling.

Rider A calmly shifts into an appropriately lower gear and goes merrily on his way. Moreover, this rider always knows, or can easily determine by a quick glance at his chain, which one of the gears he is using and how to shift to any of the remaining ones. He has a plan for shifting and knows what his next upward or downward shift is likely to be. When conditions necessitate another change he makes it and goes on enjoying himself.

Rider B guesses about which shift lever to use and finds that, instead of becoming easier, the pedaling has become even more difficult. Or perhaps the pedaling has become easier but is now too easy. He fiddles around with the levers hoping to find a comfortable gear and, if lucky, is successful and all set, but only until the next time that a change is desirable. Unfortunately this type of rider often gives up in despair and uses his beautiful multi-speed bicycle as a 1-speed, thereby foregoing much of the pleasure to be found in modern-day bicycling.

Part I of this book contains the knowledge that converts rider B to rider A!

When coupled with the machine of the human body, a modern-day light-weight bicycle (Figure 1) is capable of providing useful, inexpensive,

15

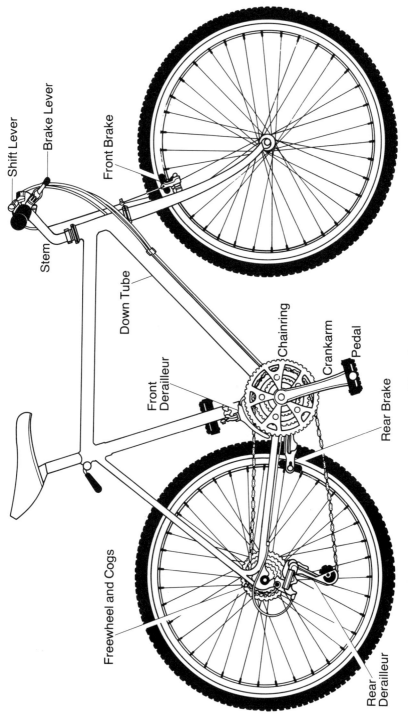

Shift Lever

Brake Lever

Front Brake

Stem

Down Tube

Front Derailleur

Chainring

Crankarm

Pedal

Rear Brake

Freewheel and Cogs

Rear Derailleur

Figure 1

nonpolluting transportation, significant aerobic benefits to the user and, perhaps most important, hours of exhilarating pleasure. This book provides you with the knowledge that enables you to take full advantage of this marvelous machine.

EXTERNAL PHYSICAL CONDITIONS

The first reason for having so many gears on your bicycle is to combat the external physical conditions of wind, hills, and road surface. When a bicycle is in a high gear each revolution of the pedals propels it a long distance, perhaps 300 inches or so — but pedaling effort is very high. High gears are used for going downhill or with the wind, on paved roads. When a bicycle is in a low gear each revolution of the pedals propels the bicycle only a short distance, perhaps even as little as 60 inches. However, the pedals are much easier to turn. Low gears are used for riding uphill or against the wind or on unpaved roads.

Every summer, thousands of people experience the adventure of bicycle touring, many pedaling coast-to-coast across the United States. Only a few are serious athletes; most are ordinary people of all ages from senior citizens to the very young. Some are even overweight, but only seldom is it necessary for these experienced bicycle tourists to walk uphill, for they all know how to use the gears on their bicycles.

Every weekend thousands of people go on day-rides, bicycling usually 10 to 100 miles in one day, and usually in a "loop," finishing where they began. They have the wind with them about half the time and use lower gears the other half of the ride, when the wind is against them. They also encounter just as many uphills as downhills and change gears accordingly. As the ride nears its end, they expect to be more tired than they were at the beginning, and to return in lower, easier gears than the ones in which they began the day.

The city/street bike version of the all-terrain bicycle has led to increased numbers of people who enjoy using bicycles for basic transportation. These riders frequently use low start-up gears after being stopped by traffic signals, and shift to higher gears soon thereafter.

Mountain bicycles, which are built for off-pavement use, put their riders in closer touch with nature and allow them to experience an even greater sense of adventure than is possible with other types of bicycles. Mountain bikes can be used successfully for riding up extremely steep hills and even on snow and ice. Many people regularly enjoy riding under these conditions, but *low gears, and the knowledge of how to use them, are essential.*

So multi-speed bicycles allow you to deal effectively with the external physical conditions that you encounter on a ride. But there is another, equally important, reason for having so many gears on your bicycle.

17

BODY OPTIONS

When riding a bicycle you make significant use of both the strength in your legs and your cardiovascular system. Multi-speed bicycles allow you to *choose* the amount of each that you use at any particular moment. Riders who regularly choose to emphasize leg strength are known as *plungers* or *mashers*, whereas those who usually emphasize the use of their cardiovascular system are called *spinners*. Beginners usually make the *wrong* choice and become plungers.

Plungers choose high (difficult) gears, which require that they push hard on the pedals, and move their feet slowly. It is now well established that *pushing hard on your pedals, as a regular way of bicycling, can quickly damage your knees!* Plungers often develop knee problems.

Spinners choose lower (easier) gears than plungers, which allows them to "spin" the pedals relatively fast, use comparatively little leg strength, and avoid the necessity of pushing so hard. Spinners rarely have knee problems.

In order to become a successful spinner you need to *learn* to feel comfortable while moving your feet relatively fast for extended periods of time. In bicycling, the number of full pedal revolutions per minute (rpm) is called *cadence*. (Cyclocomputers are available which measure cadence.) No one has difficulty achieving a cadence of 60 rpm, as this is about the same as a comfortable walking pace. But this is too low for spinning purposes. With just a moderate amount of practice, you should be able to learn to use lower gears and to increase your cadence to about 80 rpm. (If you have difficulty achieving a cadence of 80 rpm, it may be that the seat of your bicycle is positioned too low. If so, your knees have a long way to travel and your cadence is severely limited. Proper seat height calls for your knee to be just slightly bent when your pedal is at its lowest position.)

After achieving a cadence of approximately 80 rpm, you need to remember the first rule of this book, that bicycle riding should be fun. It will be easier on your knees if you can become a true spinner and increase your cadence to about 100 rpm, but this may require so much practice that you no longer enjoy riding. If so, you may wish to settle for a reduced cadence. This is a personal matter that you should decide based upon what kind of bicycling you do, how easily you are able to acquire the higher rpm's, and how much risk you are willing to take concerning possible damage to your knees.

As you ride, the gear/cadence combination that you choose affects your endurance. Choose a gear that is too high and your legs (or knees) will send a message indicating that they won't be able to continue in that gear very long. Choose a gear that is too low, which requires a cadence that is too high, and your lungs will send the same type of message. The optimum gear/cadence

combination is one in which your legs and lungs both feel as though they will
be able to continue for a long period of time.

Shifting gears can be thought of as *fine-tuning* the relationship between
your body and your bicycle in response to changing external physical
conditions. *When* to do this fine-tuning is largely determined by the external
physical conditions that you encounter and the messages that you receive
from your legs and lungs. *How* to do the fine-tuning is what you will learn
in Chapters 3-5.

SHIFTING CONVENIENCE

Another reason for having so many gears on your bicycle is to permit a
reasonably easy shift sequence. After you learn the fundamentals of gearing,
you will want to decide upon a shift sequence that will take you from your
lowest gear to your highest in a convenient, efficient manner. To do this you
may decide to avoid the use of some gears which require difficult shifts.
Generally speaking, the more gears that are on your bicycle the more
possibilities you have of finding an appropriate shift sequence that is also easy
to use. A major reason that 15- and 18-speed bicycles are so popular is that
they allow for especially low gears along with easy shifting.

2. THE FIVE BASIC PARTS

In order to understand and discuss the gearing on a multi-speed bicycle, it is necessary to become familiar with the five basic parts that produce the gears: shift levers, chainrings, cogs, front derailleur, and rear derailleur.

CHAINRINGS

The chainrings (Figure 2, also called *chainwheels* and *front sprockets*) are the toothed wheels turned by the pedals. The frontmost part of the chain goes around one of them.

The *crankset* of the bicycle consists of the chainrings and *crankarms* (Figure 2). Sometimes the crankarms and the chainrings are actually the same piece of metal; on other cranksets they are separate pieces. Different types of cranksets are discussed in Chapter 6.

On 10-, 12-, and 14-speed bicycles there are two chainrings; these are called double cranksets. On 15-, 18-, and 21-speed bicycles there are three chainrings; these are referred to as triple cranksets.

FRONT DERAILLEUR

The front derailleur (Figure 2) is located near the top of the largest chainring. The derailleur lifts the bicycle chain, which goes through it, off one chainring and puts it onto another one. A wire cable connects the front derailleur to the left shift lever.

COGS

The cogs (Figure 2, also called *rear sprockets*) are the toothed gears located in the center of the rear wheel; the rearmost part of the chain goes around one of the cogs. There are five cogs on 10- and 15-speed bicycles, six cogs on 12- and 18-speed bicycles, and seven cogs on 14- and 21-speed bicycles.

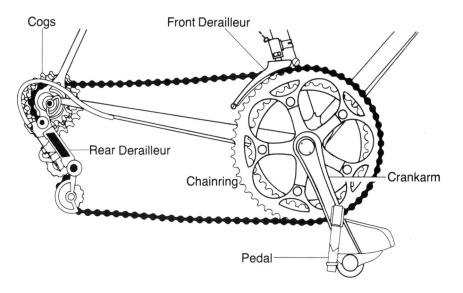

Figure 2

Frequently the cogs, taken collectively, are called the *freewheel* of the bicycle. This is technically incorrect, as the cogs, and the spacers between them, are mounted onto the actual freewheel and this entire unit is then attached to the hub of the rear wheel.

REAR DERAILLEUR

The rear derailleur (Figure 2) moves the chain from one cog to another. It is located slightly to the rear and slightly below the center of the rear wheel. The chain "snakes" through the rear derailleur.

If the rear derailleur of the bicycle becomes bent, it will not operate properly. A bent rear derailleur can also become caught in the spokes of the rear wheel, possibly causing an accident which can hurt the rider as well as damage the rear wheel and derailleur. To avoid this possibility, experienced bicyclists, when laying their bicycles down, do so with the left side down so that the rear derailleur is up, away from the ground. Sometimes a damaged rear derailleur may be re-bent to its proper position, but this should be attempted only by a qualified bicycle mechanic.

SHIFT LEVERS

There are two shift levers, one for operating each derailleur. There are four places where the shift levers might be located on your bicycle. One popular place is on the stem, near the center of the handlebars. Another is on the down-tube, the diagonal tube that runs from down near the pedals to up near the top of the front wheel. The third possibility is attached to the very ends of the handlebars. Finally, the shift levers might be attached to the top of the handlebars. This is usually the case with all-terrain bicycles or mountain bicycles, and some bicycles with upright handlebars. A cable connects each shift lever to its corresponding derailleur.

The left shift lever operates the front derailleur, the right shift lever, the rear derailleur. Move the shift levers back and forth and watch the corresponding derailleurs move in and out (left and right) as you do so. The chain, however, will not actually move from one chainring to another (or, in the rear, from one cog to another) unless you are also pedaling.

3. IDENTIFYING BICYCLE GEARS

Unlike automobiles, which have a shift lever and gear indicator (or pattern on the shift knob), bicycles have two shift levers and no indicator. On 10-speed bicycles there are 10 ways to position the two levers, but how is one to know what gear is presently being used or how to move the levers to get to a more appropriate gear? Without some type of chart, diagram, or indicator, even experienced riders are understandably confused. What riders need is something on the bicycle to indicate

(1) What size gears are on the bicycle;
(2) Which gear is presently being used; and
(3) How to move the levers to get to any other gear.

It turns out that all of this can be done fairly easily. The balance of this chapter will show you how to create such an indicator for your bicycle.

GEAR-INCH NUMBERS EXPLAINED

Each gear on your bicycle will be identified by a number called a gear-inch number. Gear-inch numbers range from a low of about 20 inches to a high of 120 inches. So instead of saying, "I am using third gear," or "Now I am in eighth gear," you will be saying something like, "I am using a 50-inch gear" or "Now I am in a 77-inch gear." This is the standard way of identifying bicycle gears in the United States. Here are the gear-inch numbers for one possible 10-speed gearing:

77	100
64	83
54	70
45	59
39	50

If you have a 10-speed bicycle, the 10 gear-inch numbers that you determine should be written in 2 columns of 5 numbers each, as illustrated. This will be called the gear-inch *matrix* for your bicycle. Since not all 10-speed bicycles have the same gearing, your matrix will probably contain different numbers than those illustrated. A step-by-step procedure for finding your gear-inch numbers, and arranging them properly, will be discussed in the next section. The arrangement is important because the location of each number will tell you how to position your chain in order to get your bicycle into that gear.

A matrix of gear-inch numbers representing one possible 12-speed gearing:

81	100
71	88
60	74
52	64
44	54
38	47

A 12-speed bicycle requires a matrix having 2 columns of 6 numbers each. (A 14-speed bicycle's matrix would have seven numbers in each column.)

If you have a 15-speed bicycle, your gear-inch matrix should have 3 columns of 5 numbers each. Here is a matrix of gear-inch numbers representing one possible 15-speed gearing:

54	84	100
44	71	83
38	61	70
32	51	58
28	45	52

In the same way, an 18-speed gearing requires a matrix having 3 columns of 6 numbers each; a 21-speed gearing is represented by a matrix having 3 columns of 7 numbers each, and so on.

STEP-BY-STEP PROCEDURE

To make the gear-inch matrix for *your* bicycle, follow these steps carefully. You should have no trouble — Steps 1 and 3 may require a small amount of time if you need to count the number of teeth on your chainrings and cogs, but the other steps are quite easy. Counting teeth on chainrings and cogs is a one-time task and a small price to pay for the added fun of knowing *exactly* how to shift from one gear to another.

STEP 1   *Determine the number of teeth on each chainring.*

There are different ways to do this. The number of teeth may be stamped right into the chainring (look on both sides, if necessary). Sometimes this information is listed in the instruction booklet for your bicycle, but most likely it will be necessary to count them. Use a pencil mark or small piece of tape to help you remember which tooth was "number one."

Counting teeth on the largest chainring is easy. For the others, you may wish to turn your bicycle upside down or to lay it on its side. If you turn it upside down, be careful not to damage the cables leading to brakes or shift levers mounted on the handlebars. If you lay it down, be careful that the rear derailleur does not become bent.

STEP 2   *Record the numbers from Step 1 on a piece of paper with the smallest number at the left and the largest at the right.*

Example

40   52

(Numbers are for example only — yours will probably differ. If you have a triple crankset, you will have three numbers to record.)

STEP 3   *Determine the number of teeth on each cog.*

You will probably have to count to do this. Sometimes these numbers are stamped into the cogs, but only rarely. If you have a new bicycle, they *might* be listed in your instruction booklet.

STEP 4   *Write the numbers from Step 3 in a column, in order, with the smallest at the top. Write the numbers from Step 1 in a row, as shown below.*

	40	52
14		
17		
20		
24		
28		

(14, 17, 20, 24, and 28 are for example only — yours will probably differ. If you have 6 cogs you will have 6 numbers to record.)

STEP 5   *Determine the diameter of the rear wheel in inches.*

This is easy to do as it is probably either 26 or 27 inches, and is usually stamped into (or printed onto) either the rim or the tire. (If you have 700-mm rims and tires, use 27 inches for the diameter.) All-terrain bikes (mountain bikes, street bikes, and city bikes) with fat tires have 26-inch wheels. If necessary, measure through the center of the wheel, from the bottom of the tire to the top of the tire. Do not expect to get exactly 26 or 27 inches, as this varies with tire pressure and other factors. But you should be close enough to determine which one is on your bicycle.

STEP 6   *Fill in the body of the chart.*

To create your gear-inch matrix, use the gear-inch numbers in either the 27-inch/700-mm chart or the 26-inch chart (pages 27 and 28). At the top of the page find the number of teeth on one of your chainrings. Along the left side find the number of teeth on one of your cogs. The table entry in that column and row gives the required gear-inch number. (The method used here is good only for 26-inch and 27-inch/700-mm wheels. If you have wheels of another size, you will need to use the formula discussed and illustrated in Appendix I.) The completed gear-inch matrix for Gearing A (having 27-inch wheels) is shown below.

A	40	52
14	77	100
17	64	83
20	54	70
24	45	59
28	39	50

Gear-inch Chart for 27-inch Wheels

Number of Teeth on Chainring

Number of Teeth on Cog	24	26	28	29	30	31	32	33	34	35	36	37	38	39	40	41	42	43	44	45	46	47	48	49	50	51	52	53	54
11	59	64	69	71	74	76	79	81	83	86	88	91	93	96	98	101	103	106	108	110	113	115	118	120	123	125	128	130	133
12	54	59	63	65	68	70	72	74	77	79	81	83	86	88	90	92	95	97	99	101	104	106	108	110	113	115	117	119	122
13	50	54	58	60	62	64	66	69	71	73	75	77	79	81	83	85	87	89	91	93	96	98	100	102	104	106	108	110	112
14	46	50	54	56	58	60	62	64	66	68	69	71	73	75	77	79	81	83	85	87	89	91	93	95	96	98	100	102	104
15	43	47	50	52	54	56	58	59	61	63	65	67	68	70	72	74	76	77	79	81	83	85	86	88	90	92	94	95	97
16	41	44	47	49	51	52	54	56	57	59	61	62	64	66	68	69	71	73	74	76	78	79	81	83	84	86	88	89	91
17	38	41	44	46	48	49	51	52	54	56	57	59	60	62	64	65	67	68	70	71	73	75	76	78	79	81	83	84	86
18	36	39	42	44	45	47	48	50	51	53	54	56	57	59	60	62	63	65	66	68	69	71	72	74	75	77	78	80	81
19	34	37	40	41	43	44	45	47	48	50	51	53	54	55	57	58	60	61	63	64	65	67	68	70	71	72	74	75	77
20	32	35	38	39	41	42	43	45	46	47	49	50	51	53	54	55	57	58	59	61	62	63	65	66	68	69	70	72	73
21	31	33	36	37	39	40	41	42	44	45	46	48	49	50	51	53	54	55	57	58	59	60	62	63	64	66	67	68	69
22	29	32	34	36	37	38	39	41	42	43	44	45	47	48	49	50	52	53	54	55	56	58	59	60	61	63	64	65	66
23	28	31	33	34	35	36	38	39	40	41	42	43	45	46	47	48	49	50	52	53	54	55	56	58	59	60	61	62	63
24	27	29	32	33	34	35	36	37	38	39	41	42	43	44	45	46	47	48	50	51	52	53	54	55	56	57	59	60	61
25	26	28	30	31	32	33	35	36	37	38	39	40	41	42	43	44	45	46	48	49	50	51	52	53	54	55	56	57	58
26	25	27	29	30	31	32	33	34	35	36	37	38	39	41	42	43	44	45	46	47	48	49	50	51	52	53	54	55	56
27	24	26	28	29	30	31	32	33	34	35	36	37	38	39	40	41	42	43	44	45	46	47	48	49	50	51	52	53	54
28	23	25	27	28	29	30	31	32	33	34	35	36	37	38	39	40	41	41	42	43	44	45	46	47	48	49	50	51	52
29	22	24	26	27	28	29	30	31	32	33	34	34	35	36	37	38	39	40	41	42	43	44	45	46	47	47	48	49	50
30	22	23	25	26	27	28	29	30	31	32	32	33	34	35	36	37	38	39	40	41	41	42	43	44	45	46	47	48	49
31	21	23	24	25	26	27	28	29	30	30	31	32	33	34	35	36	37	37	38	39	40	41	42	43	44	44	45	46	47
32	20	22	24	24	25	26	27	28	29	30	30	31	32	33	34	35	35	36	37	38	39	40	41	41	42	43	44	45	46
33	20	21	23	24	25	25	26	27	28	29	29	30	31	32	33	34	34	35	36	37	38	38	39	40	41	42	43	43	44
34	19	21	22	23	24	25	25	26	27	28	29	29	30	31	32	33	33	34	35	36	37	37	38	39	40	41	41	42	43

Gear-inch Chart for 26-inch Wheels

Number of Teeth on Chainring

Number of Teeth on Cog	24	26	28	29	30	31	32	33	34	35	36	37	38	39	40	41	42	43	44	45	46	47	48	49	50	51	52	53	54
11	57	61	66	69	71	73	76	78	80	83	85	87	90	92	95	97	99	102	104	106	109	111	113	116	118	121	123	125	128
12	52	56	61	63	65	67	69	72	74	76	78	80	82	85	87	89	91	93	95	98	100	102	104	106	108	111	113	115	117
13	48	52	56	58	60	62	64	66	68	70	72	74	76	78	80	82	84	86	88	90	92	94	96	98	100	102	104	106	108
14	45	48	52	54	56	58	59	61	63	65	67	69	71	72	74	76	78	80	82	84	85	87	89	91	93	95	97	98	100
15	42	45	49	50	52	54	55	57	59	61	62	64	66	68	69	71	73	75	76	78	80	81	83	85	87	88	90	92	94
16	39	42	46	47	49	50	52	54	55	57	59	60	62	63	65	67	68	70	72	73	75	76	78	80	81	83	85	86	88
17	37	40	43	44	46	47	49	50	52	54	55	57	58	60	61	63	64	66	67	69	70	72	73	75	76	78	80	81	83
18	35	38	40	42	43	45	46	48	49	51	52	53	55	56	58	59	61	62	64	65	66	68	69	71	72	74	75	77	78
19	33	36	38	40	41	42	44	45	47	48	49	51	52	53	55	56	57	59	60	62	63	64	66	67	68	70	71	73	74
20	31	34	36	38	39	40	42	43	44	46	47	48	49	51	52	53	55	56	57	59	60	61	62	64	65	66	68	69	70
21	30	32	35	36	37	38	40	41	42	43	45	46	47	48	50	51	52	53	54	56	57	58	59	61	62	63	64	66	67
22	28	31	34	34	35	37	38	39	40	41	43	44	45	46	47	48	50	51	52	53	54	56	57	58	59	60	61	63	64
23	27	29	32	33	34	35	36	37	38	40	41	42	43	44	45	46	47	49	50	51	52	53	54	55	57	58	59	60	61
24	26	28	30	31	33	34	35	36	37	38	39	40	41	42	43	44	46	47	48	49	50	51	52	53	54	55	56	57	59
25	25	27	29	30	31	32	33	34	35	36	37	38	40	41	42	43	44	45	46	47	48	49	50	51	52	53	54	55	56
26	24	26	28	29	30	31	32	33	34	35	36	37	38	39	40	41	42	43	44	45	46	47	48	49	50	51	52	53	54
27	23	25	27	28	29	30	31	32	33	34	35	36	37	38	39	39	40	41	42	43	44	45	46	47	48	49	50	51	52
28	22	24	26	27	28	29	30	31	32	33	33	34	35	36	37	38	39	40	41	42	43	44	45	46	46	47	48	49	50
29	22	23	25	26	27	28	29	30	30	31	32	33	34	35	36	37	38	39	39	40	41	42	43	44	45	46	47	48	48
30	21	23	24	25	26	27	28	29	29	30	31	32	33	34	35	36	36	37	38	39	40	41	42	42	43	44	45	46	47
31	20	22	23	24	25	26	27	28	29	29	30	31	32	33	34	34	35	36	37	38	39	39	40	41	42	43	44	44	45
32	20	21	23	24	24	25	26	27	28	28	29	30	31	32	33	33	34	35	36	37	37	38	39	40	41	41	42	43	44
33	19	20	22	23	24	24	25	26	27	28	28	29	30	31	32	32	33	34	35	35	36	37	38	39	39	40	41	42	43
34	18	20	21	22	23	24	24	25	26	27	28	28	29	30	31	31	32	33	34	34	35	36	37	37	38	39	40	41	41

Gearing A was chosen for use in the example because it is a common gearing for inexpensive 10-speed bicycles. The same size chainrings and cogs also occur on many bicycles having 26-inch wheels. For the convenience of those readers who have this gearing and wheel combination, the completed matrix is provided below, labeled as Gearing B.

B	40	52
14	74	97
17	61	80
20	52	68
24	43	56
28	37	48

Gearing B (26-inch wheels)

In this book, gearings resulting from 26-inch wheels will be clearly labeled as such. **But if no indication of the wheel size is given, the gearing is for 27-inch/700-mm wheels.**

STEP 7   *Reproduce the body (just the gear-inch numbers) of your chart onto the appropriate form of Appendix L.*

Since the bicycle in the example (Gearing A) is a 10-speed, the Appendix L form which has 5 rows and 2 columns is chosen and filled in as shown below.

77	100
64	83
54	70
45	59
39	50

STEP 8   *Tape the copy of the gear-inch matrix that you made in Step 7 to your bicycle in a place that is easy to see,* perhaps on the top of the stem, in back of the center of the handlebars (Figure 3). Clear plastic tape is rainproof and works well, although any transparent tape will do.

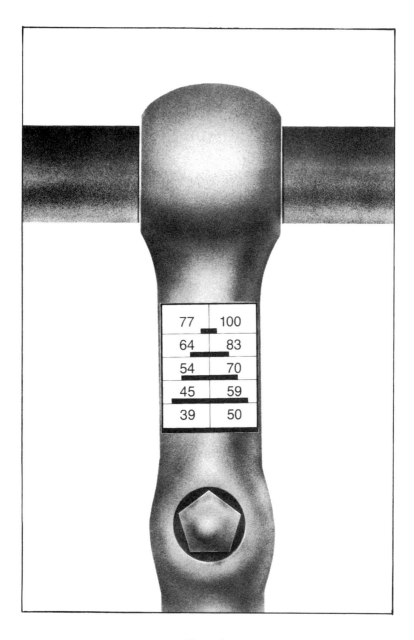

Figure 3

STEP 9   *Make a copy of the gearing chart for your bicycle and save it for future reference.*

Use the chart of Step 6 which includes the chainring and cog tooth numbers. Counting teeth is somewhat time-consuming and messy and you do not want to have to do it again.

LOCATING EACH GEAR

Each gear-inch number's position in the matrix indicates how to arrange your chain to select that gear. For example, to select the 70-inch gear in Gearing A, the chain must be positioned on the 52-tooth chainring and the 20-tooth cog, as shown below

A	40	(52)
14	77	100
17	64	83
(20)	54	(70)
24	45	59
28	39	50

If riding in the 70-inch gear becomes too difficult (that is, pedal effort is too high), you might shift to the 24-tooth rear cog (right shift lever) and try the 59-inch gear.

A	40	(52)
14	77	100
17	64	83
20	54	70
(24)	45	(59)
28	39	50

If the 59-inch gear turns out to be too low, look for a gear that is between 59 and 70 inches. The chart indicates that there is a 64-inch gear on this bicycle, and to achieve it a *double-shift* must be performed: Shift the chain to the 40-tooth chainring (left shift lever, front derailleur) and the 17-tooth cog (right lever, rear derailleur), as shown below.

A	(40)	52
14	77	100
(17)	(64)	83
20	54	70
24	45	59
28	39	50

As you ride, you don't need to know how many teeth are on each chainring or on each cog. The left column of numbers tells you to use the left chainring, the middle column (if you have one) is for the middle chainring, and the right column is for the right chainring.

The gears resulting from the cog with the smallest number of teeth (producing the higher, harder gears) are at the top of the matrix, while those using the cog with the largest number of teeth (lower, easier gears) are at the bottom. The form of Appendix L, which you used in Step 7, is designed to help you remember this, especially if you are a beginner or don't ride very often. This form contains heavy horizontal lines which represent the cogs of your bicycle. In the example illustrated in Figure 4, the 77- and 100-inch gears are located near the smallest heavy line, which means that the smallest cog must be used to achieve these gears. The 39- and 50-inch gears are located near the largest heavy line, and so the largest cog must be used to obtain these gears.

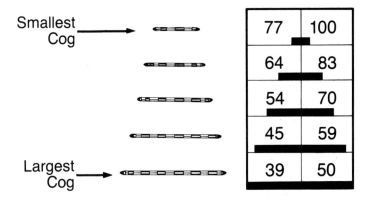

Figure 4

THE DEFINITION OF A GEAR-INCH NUMBER

In any gear-inch matrix it is the *relative sizes* of the numbers, along with their positions, that is important. In the previous example, it was observed that if the 70-inch gear felt too difficult but the 59-inch gear felt too easy, the 64-inch gear would probably feel comfortable. So you really don't need to know what is meant by a 59-inch gear, a 64-inch gear, or a 70-inch gear in order to use your matrix effectively.

But in case you do wish to know the meaning of a gear-inch number, the following brief explanation is provided. If you multiply the gear-inch number of the gear that you are using by pi, you will get the number of inches that your bicycle moves forward every time your feet go around once (assuming, of course, that you are not coasting).

If you are in a 59-inch gear, every revolution of your feet propels your bicycle 59 times pi inches (which is about 185 inches since pi is approximately 3.14). If you are in a 70-inch gear, every revolution of your feet propels your bicycle 70 times pi (or about 220) inches.

4. BASIC INFORMATION ABOUT SHIFTING

Now that you have your gear-inch matrix taped to your bicycle, you can tell what size gears are available and how to position your chain to get your bicycle into each gear. This chapter provides other basic information that you should know in order to shift gears properly and use your bicycle safely.

IMPORTANT WARNINGS

(1) *Carefully consider WHEN to look at your chain, as looking at your chain can be mesmerizing.* (Some bicyclists have run into *parked* cars while staring at their chains.)

A quick glance straight down easily determines which chainring you are using; to see which cog your chain is on, you need to look down and back, through your legs. At the beginning you might find yourself taking a few seconds to do this, especially if you have six cogs and your chain is on one of the two in the center.

Don't look at your chain when you are riding in heavy traffic or when you are riding close behind a car or another bicycle. Remember that *you don't know what the vehicle in front of you is going to do. It is unsafe to assume that it will continue at its present rate of speed.* If it slows down while you are looking at your chain, you could go flying head-first over your bicycle. Slow down, drop back a safe distance, and then look at your chain.

Even if there are no other vehicles around, check the road surface ahead of you. Looking at your chain can wait a few seconds until you are safely past those bumps or potholes in the road.

(2) *Avoid back-pedaling, especially when shifting.*

Most rear derailleurs are one-way devices, designed to accommodate forward pedaling only. Back-pedaling can result in serious damage to your rear derailleur.

(3) *Don't try to shift gears when your chain is under a severe strain.*

Attempting to shift when your chain is under a severe strain can result in bent or broken derailleurs and cogs. When pedaling hard, as when going uphill, ease off a little on the pedaling before attempting to shift gears. (In recent years manufacturers have improved the quality of front and rear derailleurs so that this problem is not as serious as it was in the past, but there is still a limit to the amount of strain that can be tolerated when shifting.)

Sometimes even experienced riders get caught going uphill in a gear that is too high and are unable to shift to a lower gear because of the strain on the chain. When this occurs, the best procedure is to *STOP!* Don't risk damaging your knees by trying to go uphill in a gear that is too high, and don't risk breaking parts of your bicycle by trying to shift. If you don't want to walk your bicycle up the hill, then turn around, pedal downhill for a few yards and, while there is no strain on your chain, shift to a lower gear. Then turn around again and continue safely uphill.

(4) *Don't purposely shift the chain over too many cogs at once.*

As a general rule, it is best to momentarily pause at each cog before shifting to the next one. If there is little or no strain on your chain you will probably be able to shift at will, without pausing. But as the strain on your chain increases so does the risk that you will damage your rear derailleur or some cogs by attempting to shift over more than one cog without pausing.

(5) *Don't move both shift levers at the same time.*

This can "throw the chain" (i.e., the chain comes off the sprockets).

INDEXED SHIFTING SYSTEMS

Originally developed for mountain bikes, indexed systems are rapidly becoming standard equipment on all kinds of multi-speed bicycles. An indexed shifting system is one in which you can hear and feel the shift levers "click" into place. To achieve the precision necessary for this type of shifting, the shift levers, front and rear derailleur, chainrings, cogs, chain, cables, and cable housings must all be designed to work perfectly with one another, and this is why they are referred to as *systems*. Different manufacturers have their own systems, and individual components from one system usually may not be replaced with those of another system.

For an indexed shifting system to function correctly it is necessary that the components be *adjusted* properly. Of particular concern are the cables, as new cables *always* stretch a little until they settle into their final lengths. Since a cable stretch of just 1 millimeter can cause an indexed shifting system to function poorly, do not be discouraged if the system on your new bicycle does not work properly, as it probably just needs adjusting. The dealer will probably tell you to return it for proper adjustment.

Indexed shifting systems provide you with the option of turning off the indexed feature and using the levers in the alternate friction mode (explained in more detail in the next section). This enables you to temporarily replace a broken component with one which is incompatible with your indexed system and still be able to use your bicycle. It also allows you to use your bicycle when the indexed system needs adjustment, which will be the case whenever you are unable to complete a shift or hear a strange noise from your front or rear derailleur. So even if your bicycle has indexed shifting, read the next section — you may need it someday.

FRICTION SHIFT LEVERS

Friction shift levers, as opposed to indexed (or "click") shifting systems, use friction to keep your shift levers (and the derailleurs) in the positions that you have placed them. The friction is provided by a bolt at each shift lever. If one of these bolts is too tight you will be unable to move that shift lever. But if the bolt is too loose it will not provide enough friction to overcome the spring in the derailleur, and the derailleur will not remain where you positioned it. So if your bicycle shifts gears "all by itself," you probably need to tighten the bolt at the proper shift lever. (Sometimes frame-flex will cause a shift in gears with friction shift levers.)

Friction shift levers have been in use for many years and work quite well, but a certain amount of practice is required to learn to use them properly. This is because it is usually necessary to move a friction shift lever in *two* directions in order to complete each shift. If you move the lever in only one direction you will get either front or rear derailleur noise.

Derailleur Noise

A distinct "clack, clack, clack, ..." coming from your rear derailleur means that the cage of your rear derailleur (the part that moves) is improperly positioned between two cogs instead of being located directly beneath the cog that is being used, as it should be. To eliminate this annoying (and eventually harmful) sound, simply move the right shift lever a slight amount in whichever direction is required to position the cage properly and eliminate the noise. If you move the shift lever too far, or in the wrong direction, the worst that can happen is that you will shift gears. So shift back and try again.

Rear derailleur noise occurs whenever you shift with the rear derailleur using only one movement of your right lever; it is necessary for the cage to move slightly past the next cog before the chain will shift onto that cog. To complete the shift you need to move the cage back a little so that it will be positioned directly underneath the new cog.

Immediately after making the first lever movement and causing your chain to shift, *listen* to your rear derailleur. If there is too much noise, as there probably will be, move your lever back just slightly. Eventually making this second lever movement becomes a habit.

In the same way, front derailleur noise is a scraping sound caused by the chain rubbing against one of the sides of the front derailleur. To eliminate this noise simply move the left shift lever slightly, so that the chain passes between the sides of the front derailleur without touching them.

Front derailleur noise can also occur immediately after a shift with the *rear* derailleur. This is because the rear derailleur moves the chain left or right, which may cause the chain to touch one of the sides of the front derailleur. Reposition the front derailleur accordingly. Some front derailleurs are designed with a wide opening at the rear specifically to reduce the occurrence of front derailleur noise after a shift with the rear derailleur.

PRACTICE AT SHIFTING

If you are a beginning rider it will be appropriate for you to have a short practice session to learn what it feels like to shift, and to see if the gearing components of your bicycle are working properly. Take your bicycle to a place where it will be safe to frequently look down at your chain. Empty school, church, or shopping center parking lots are good places for this, as is any seldom used, but well paved, *level* stretch of road.

USING YOUR FRONT DERAILLEUR

While pedaling, shift the chain to one of the center cogs and leave it there for awhile. Then shift the chain back and forth a few times through each of the two or three chainrings. As you make each shift you will feel the pedaling become easier or harder, but look at the chain anyway (when it is safe to do so) to see where it is located. If you have friction levers *listen* and *look* for front derailleur noise and shift back just a little to eliminate the noise. If you have indexed shifting, practice in both the indexed and friction modes so that you will feel prepared to use either one. You should begin to develop the feeling that you know what is happening when you use your left shift lever.

USING YOUR REAR DERAILLEUR

Shift the chain to the smaller of the two (or middle of your three) chainrings and leave it there as you practice shifting with your rear derailleur. Then try shifting your chain onto each of your cogs without skipping any, and frequently look to see if you have been successful. With indexed shifting this should be easy to do; you should also try using the friction mode.

With friction shift levers it will probably take a certain amount of practice before you are able to shift from one cog to another without skipping any. It is unnecessary to master this skill now, but with just a moderate amount of practice you should "get the feel" of your rear derailleur and become reasonably successful at shifting the chain over only one cog.

MECHANICAL PROBLEMS

Good shifting requires that your gearing components be clean and lubricated. Derailleurs have joints that move as you shift; if these joints are clogged with dirt or rust, shifting is difficult. The cables need to move freely within their housings — if they do not you may not be able to shift at all. It also helps to have the chainrings, cogs, and chain reasonably clean.

If your gearing components are clean and lubricated, and your chain won't shift onto the largest or smallest chainring or onto the largest or smallest cog, most likely one or both of your derailleurs need adjusting. Each derailleur has two adjusting screws which impose physical limits on how far to the outside or inside the chain is allowed to go. But turning these screws too far can cause your chain to shift completely off all of the chainrings or cogs, and so you may wish to consult a bicycle mechanic or a book on bicycle repair.

If your indexed shift levers click into place but your chain does not shift, most likely your system needs adjusting, and you should take your bicycle to a qualified mechanic.

A BEGINNING STRATEGY OF SHIFTING

A good beginning strategy of shifting is to find a comfortable, favorite gear and use only the one chainring that involves that gear for awhile. Try to find a gear from about 50 to 70 inches that feels comfortable on level, paved roads and call it your *base gear.* If you have three chainrings, the ideal situation would be to have your base gear in the center of your matrix, so that it uses the middle chainring and the middle (or one of the two middle) cogs. For discussion purposes, suppose that your bicycle has the 10-speed gearing illustrated below and you have chosen the 54-inch gear as your base gear.

77	100
64	83
(54)	70
45	59
39	50

Start each ride in the base gear and say to yourself, "I'm riding in my favorite 54-inch gear." Whenever this feels uncomfortable, shift to another gear, but for now use only the chainring containing your base gear.

Each time you shift, look at your matrix and silently tell yourself the gear-inch number of the gear that you are using. For example, if you are riding into the wind you might say, "The 54-inch gear is too hard, I'll try the 45-inch gear." When the pedaling becomes easier you might say, "Now I'll go back to the 54-inch gear." If you encounter a slight downhill you might say, "Now I"m going to try the 64-inch gear." Soon you will find that you are becoming familiar with the gears on the chainring containing your base gear. *You will develop confidence in your ability to shift gears and a feeling that you are in control of the situation.*

At this point you will be ready to begin using the other chainring(s) on your bicycle. It will happen naturally. You will encounter physical conditions in which one gear is too high but the next lower gear on that same chainring is too low (see below).

	77	100	
Too high	(64)	89	
Too low	(54)	70	
	45	(59)	Just right
	39	50	

You will look at your matrix to see if you have a gear on another chainring that is more appropriate and find yourself shifting to it, and soon you will start to become familiar with some of the gears on each of your chainrings. *Congratulations, you are no longer a beginner!* (But be sure to read at least one more chapter, as you can add considerably to your enjoyment by developing a personal shifting strategy.)

5. DEVELOPING A PERSONAL STRATEGY OF SHIFTING

A *predetermined plan* of shifting is a *strategy* of shifting. Having a personal strategy adds to your fun because it frees your mind to think about the pleasures of riding rather than the necessities of shifting. When you need to shift to another gear, you don't need to decide which gear to use because that decision was made in advance, as part of your strategy; you only need to think about how to move the levers to accomplish the shift. And as you become more practiced at using your own strategy, you make the correct lever movements somewhat automatically, and do even less conscious thinking about your shifting. This results in a highly effective use of your gears as you think about scenery (while touring), or how to stay on course, upright, and pedaling (if you're riding off-pavement).

SINGLE- AND DOUBLE-SHIFTS

Whenever you use one of your shift levers, but not both, to change gears, you make a *single-shift*. A single-shift with your left lever moves your chain onto a different chainring, which results in a left or right movement within your matrix. The new gear is in the same row as the old gear, but is in a different column.

A single-shift with your right lever moves your chain onto a different cog and results in an up or down movement within your matrix. The new gear is in the same column, but in a different row than the old gear. Single-shifts are easy to perform, and patterns of shifting which contain only single-shifts are relatively easy to learn.

41

When you use *both* levers (one at a time, or you might throw the chain) to shift from one gear to another you make a *double-shift*. Each double-shift results in a diagonal movement within your matrix, because you change both the column *and* the row to get to the new gear. A 1-cog double-shift is illustrated below.

```
77      100
64       83
(54)     70
45      (59)
39       50
```

A *2-cog double-shift* is a double-shift that moves the chain over two cogs, such as the shift between the 59- and 64-inch gears shown below. These unpleasant shifts are usually avoided.

```
77      100
(64)     83
54       70
45      (59)
39       50
```

CATEGORIES OF GEAR-INCH CHANGES

In an effective shifting strategy the *size of change* that you make when shifting between gears is important. Certain changes are inappropriate because they are too large — others because they are too small.

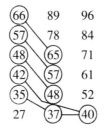

This gearing contains much duplication.

Gearings that contain gears differing by 1, 2, or 3 gear-inches are said to have *duplication,* because these changes feel nearly identical to the rider. If pedaling in a 66-inch gear is too hard, it does not help much to shift to a 65-inch gear; a larger change is needed.

A change of 4 through 8 gear-inches is called a *half-step of change.* (Changes of this size occur frequently in a type of gearing known as a Half-step gearing.) Half-steps are large enough to be felt by your body and are especially useful in the middle of your shift sequence, which contains the gears used most frequently.

A change of 9 through 14 gear-inches is called a *full-step* of change. Full-steps are often used near the low end of your shift sequence, such as up steep hills, when rapidly increasing difficulty requires more drastic measures.

Changes of 15 or more inches, while sometimes appropriate, often result in the feeling that you have made too much change.

CHAIN DEFLECTION

Chain deflection (also called *chain angle*) is lateral, or sideways, movement of your chain, and occurs whenever the chain is positioned on a chainring and cog that are in different vertical planes from one another. *Extreme chain deflection* (Figure 5) occurs whenever you use the gear which connects (A) the left chainring to the right cog (the gear in the upper left corner of your matrix), or (B) the right chainring to the left cog (the gear in the lower right corner of your matrix).

During extreme chain deflection the sides of the links rub more tightly against one another than they do when there is little or no deflection. This results in added friction, which not only causes the chain to wear out faster, but also requires that you supply extra energy to propel your bicycle. There is nothing wrong with an occasional use of the gears in the extreme chain deflection positions on a 10- or 12-speed bicycle, but it is a good idea to avoid the regular use of these gears. (If your favorite gear on your 10- or 12-speed bicycle is in an extreme chain deflection position, and you do not want to change the gearing on your bicycle, then go ahead and use it. Nothing disastrous will happen.)

On 15-, 18-, or 21-speed bicycles the extreme chain deflection is greater than on other bicycles, and should be avoided. Fortunately, on bicycles with triple cranksets, the gears in the extreme chain deflection positions are almost always duplicated elsewhere in the gearing (see below); so *extreme chain deflection should never be necessary on a 15-, 18-, or 21-speed bicycle.*

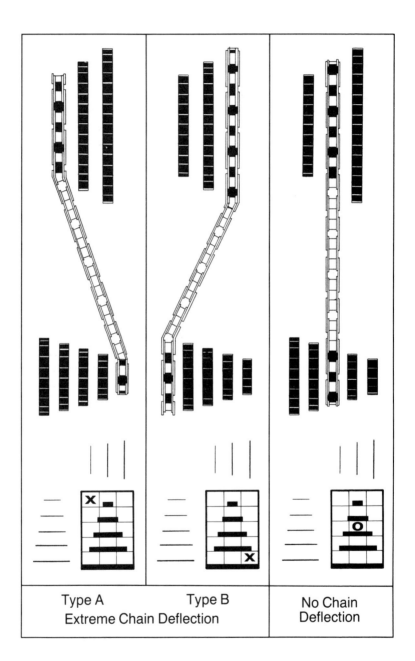

Type A   Type B
Extreme Chain Deflection

No Chain
Deflection

Figure 5

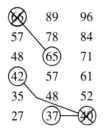

	89	96
57	78	84
48	65	71
42	57	61
35	48	52
27	37	

STRATEGY SELECTION PROCESS

The following steps are recommended for examining a gearing and selecting a shifting strategy to be used with it.

(1) Examine the gearing for duplications.

(2) Observe the gear-inch numbers of the highest and lowest gears;

(3) Examine each column, looking for half- and full-step changes;

(4) Examine each row, looking for half- and full-step changes (these provide you with opportunities to change columns using single-shifts);

(5) Select a base, or favorite, gear to be used on level pavement.

(6) Look for a *primary shift sequence* which contains the highest, lowest, and base gears, and has the following properties:

    (a) Contains as few double-shifts as possible;

    (b) Uses half- and full-step changes whenever possible;

    (c) Avoids the extreme chain deflection gears, if possible.

(7) Look for *secondary gears* which are not in the primary shift sequence but which might be useful.

SOME SAMPLE STRATEGIES

While only one strategy *especially* for off-pavement riding is listed, mountain-bikers should not skip the others; all contain tips useful for all kinds of riding.

STRATEGIES FOR GEARING A (10-SPEED)

The first gearing to be examined is the 10-speed Gearing A, shown below. Some observations about Gearing A:

A	40	52
14	77	100
17	64	83
20	54	70
24	45	59
28	39	50

(1)   There is no duplication.

(2)   Its lowest gear is a 39-inch gear; many people would like to have a lower gear for climbing steep hills. For purposes other than racing, the 100-inch gear is sufficiently high for a highest gear.

(3)   The left column contains full-step changes (45-54, 54-64, 64-77) except for the 39-45 half-step of change. The right column contains full-step changes (50-59, 59-70, 70-83) except for the 83-100 jump, which is a bit large.

(4)   Possible places to single-shift between columns are at 39-50 (a full-step of change), 45-59 (another full-step of change), and possibly 54-70. (Half-steps of change would be acceptable also, if there were any.)

(5)   Possible base gears are the 54-, 59-, 64-, and 70-inch gears.

Seven different strategies will be suggested for Gearing A, none of which is recommended as being better than the others. Choose a strategy that appeals to you and stick with it. In each strategy the primary sequence is outlined and the secondary gears are circled, as in Strategy A below.

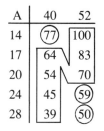

A	40	52
14	(77)	100
17	64	83
20	54	70
24	45	(59)
28	39	(50)

Strategy A

If one of the 54-, 64-, or 70-inch gears has been chosen as the base gear, the primary shift sequence could be 39-45-54-64-70-83-100, which contains only the one 64-70 1-cog double-shift. Secondary considerations are that the 50-, 59-, and 77-inch gears are on the bicycle; be willing to double-shift to achieve them whenever necessary.

If, on the other hand, the 59-inch gear has been chosen as the base gear, the 39-50-59-70-83-100 sequence, which contains no double-shifts, could be used as a primary sequence. If you have chosen the 59-inch gear as a favorite gear, the chances are that you will also like the 50-inch gear, and cannot avoid the fact that it is in an extreme chain deflection position. The 45-, 54-, 64-, and 77-inch gears could be used as secondary gears. An example, called Strategy B, is shown below.

A	40	52
14	(77)	100
17	(64)	83
20	(54)	70
24	(45)	59
28	39	50

Strategy B

Strategy C is the traditional *Double-shift Crossover* strategy for Gearing A, and consists of two sequences rather than one. With this strategy you stay in the left column until you need higher gears and then double-shift 77-83 to the right column. Once in the right column, you stay there until you need lower gears and then double-shift 50-45 to the left column. See below.

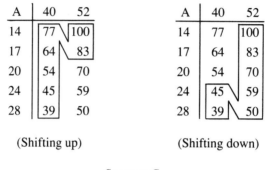

A	40	52		A	40	52
14	77	100		14	77	100
17	64	83		17	64	83
20	54	70		20	54	70
24	45	59		24	45	59
28	39	50		28	39	50

(Shifting up)   (Shifting down)

Strategy C

The 39-45-54-70-83-100 sequence shown below as Strategy D is known as the *Single-shift Crossover* sequence for this gearing. It begins with the lowest gear, goes up the left column, *crosses over at the middle row,* and continues up the right column to the highest gear. The other gears may be used as secondary gears. This strategy is *not* recommended for this particular gearing because many recreational riders would like to have either the 59- or 64-inch gear in the primary shift sequence. Also, the 54-70 change is too large to have right in the middle of the sequence.

A	40	52
14	77	100
17	64	83
20	54	70
24	45	59
28	39	50

Strategy D

Strategies E, F, and G, below, illustrate three other possibilities for this gearing; in each case the primary sequence is outlined and the secondary gears are circled.

48

A	40	52
14	(77)	100
17	(64)	83
20	(54)	70
24	45	59
28	39	(50)

Strategy E

A	40	52
14	(77)	100
17	(64)	83
20	54	70
24	45	59
28	39	(50)

Strategy F

A	40	52
14	77	100
17	64	83
20	54	(70)
24	45	(59)
28	39	(50)

Strategy G

STRATEGIES FOR GEARING C (12-SPEED)

Observations about the 12-speed Gearing C (below) are:

C	42	52
14	81	100
16	71	88
19	60	74
22	52	64
26	44	54
30	38	47

(1)   The 44- and 47-inch gears constitute a duplication, as do the 52- and 54-inch gears, and the 71- and 74-inch gears.

(2)   It ranges from a low of 38 inches to a high of 100 inches.

(3)   The left column contains 38-44, 44-52, and 52-60 half-step changes, and 60-71, 71-81 full-step changes. After the 47-54 half-step, the right column contains full-step changes.

(4)   Possible places to single-shift between columns are at 38-47, 44-54, 52-64, and 60-74. The 71-88 and 81-100 single-shifts would be too large to put into a primary shift sequence.

(5)   Possible base gears are the 52-, 54-, 60-, 64-, and perhaps 71-inch gears.

Because of the four possible single-shifts between columns, there are 4 possible single-shift primary sequences, as illustrated in strategies A, B, C, and D.

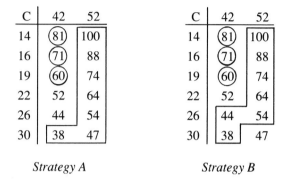

	C	42	52
14	(81)	100
16	(71)	88
19	(60)	74
22	52	64
26	44	54
30	38	47

Strategy A   Strategy B

Strategies C and D are the two Single-shift Crossover strategies for this gearing; the crossover between chainrings is made when using either of the two center cogs.

Strategy C   Strategy D

(Single-shift Crossover)   (Single-shift Crossover)

Strategy E, called a *Dual-option Crossover* strategy, is a combination of the two Single-shift Crossover strategies C and D, as it amounts to delaying the decision whether to cross over between chainrings at 52-64 or at 60-74. At those times when the 64-inch gear seems more useful than the 60, the 52-64 crossover is used; when the 60-inch gear seems preferable, the 60-74 crossover is chosen, as shown below.

C	42	52
14	(81)	100
16	(71)	88
19	60	74
22	52	64
26	44	54
30	38	47

Strategy E

(Dual-option Crossover)

The traditional Double-shift Crossover strategy F, shown below, is to stay in the left column until higher gears are needed and then double-shift 81-88 to the right column. Once in the right column you stay there until you need lower gears and then double-shift 47-44 to the left column.

C	42	52
14	81	100
16	71	88
19	60	74
22	52	64
26	44	54
30	38	47

C	42	52
14	81	100
16	71	88
19	60	74
22	52	64
26	44	54
30	38	47

(Shifting up)   (Shifting down)

Strategy F (Double-shift Crossover)

Gearings A and C illustrate a typical difference between 10- and 12-speed gearings. For a 10-speed gearing the only Single-shift Crossover strategy is somewhat ineffective because of the large gap between columns at the middle row (Gearing A, Strategy D), which makes the Double-shift Crossover strategy more appealing (Gearing A, Strategy C). For a 12-speed gearing the *three* possible Single-shift Crossover strategies (Gearing C, Strategies C, D, and E) frequently *are* effective; the Double-shift Crossover strategy (Gearing C, Strategy F) is seldom needed.

STRATEGIES FOR GEARING D (15-SPEED)

With a 15-speed gearing it is possible to have a lowest gear that is lower than that on a 10- or 12-speed gearing, but without relinquishing easy shifting. Observe the 15-speed Gearing D, below.

D	28	45	52
14	54	87	100
17	44	71	83
20	38	61	70
24	32	51	58
28	27	43	50

(1)   The 54- and 50-inch gears in the extreme chain deflection positions are duplicated in the 51-inch gear. Other duplications are 43-44, 58-61, and 70-71.

(2)   It ranges from a low of 27 inches to a high of 100 inches.

(3)   Within each of the columns, all of the changes are either half- or full-step changes except the 71-87 change in the middle column and the 83-100 change in the right column.

(4)   There is no nice single-shift between the left and center columns, as each such shift would result in a change of 16 or more inches; a double-shift will be necessary between these columns. This is often the case with 15- and 18-speed gearings because of the extremely small chain-ring that is chosen to produce the lowest gear. Between the center and right columns, all five possible single-shifts are appropriate, as they all result in changes of 7 to 13 inches.

(5)   On a 15-speed gearing, the ideal place to have your base gear is in the center of the matrix, like the 61-inch gear. This position involves *no* chain deflection and allows for easy shifting to higher and lower gears. Anyone who rarely uses a 61-inch gear might wish to consider changing to another gearing. For discussion purposes, it will be assumed that the 61-inch gear has been chosen as the base gear.

Strategy A illustrates some of the advantages of 15-speed over 12-speed gearings, and how to make best use of them. See below.

D	28	45	52
14	54	87	100
17	44	71	83
20	(38)	61	70
24	32	51	58
28	27	43	50

Strategy A

To go up from the 61-inch base gear: The 71-inch gear is a better choice than the 70 because it allows you to single-shift to either of the 83- or 87-inch gears, as appropriate.

To go down from the 61-inch gear: A reasonable sequence is 61-51-43-32-27, with the 1-cog double-shift at 43-32. The 38-inch gear might be especially useful if the 43-32 downshift is too much change.

Strategy B avoids the 43-32 downward double-shift of Strategy A. You are trying to shift to a lower gear because the pedaling is difficult; it would be better to temporarily pass through the lower 27-inch gear (left lever first) than the higher 51-inch gear (right lever first). But knowing that 27 and 32 are fairly close to one another, you might train yourself to pause a moment and try the 27-inch gear; if it feels comfortable you can remain in it, and avoid the double-shift.

D	28	45	52
14	54	87	100
17	44	71	83
20	(38)	61	70
24	(32)	51	58
28	27	43	50

Strategy B

Strategy C for Gearing D is to double-shift 51-38, and use the 44-inch gear as a secondary gear, as shown. The advantage of Strategy A over Strategy C is that it delays the double-shift as long as possible. Assuming the 61-inch gear is used often, Strategy A provides two lower gears of 51 and 43 inches before the double-shift is needed; Strategy C provides only the one 51-inch gear before it is necessary to double-shift.

D	28	45	52
14	54	87	100
17	(44)	71	83
20	38	61	70
24	32	51	58
28	27	43	50

Strategy C

START-UP GEARS

If you ride in congested areas, it is convenient to have a start-up gear that you can use immediately after being stopped at traffic signals. (A start-up gear can also be handy for mountain-bike situations like turning a sharp corner and finding "heart attack hill" dead ahead.) 15- and 18-speed gearings provide an especially nice place to have such a gear: in the left column, just next to the base gear, like the 38-inch gear in Gearing D, below.

D	28	45	52
14	54	87	100
17	44	71	83
20	(38)—61		70
24	32	51	58
28	27	43	50

The 38-inch gear is a particularly nice start-up gear; it is about the right size in relation to the base gear. If you feel comfortable riding in the 61-inch gear, the 38-inch gear should feel good as a start-up gear.

Another reason for using the 38-inch gear for start-up purposes (while riding in the 61-inch gear) is that your front derailleur usually provides a nice, clean shift. If you have friction levers and use your rear derailleur to shift into or out of a start-up gear, you can often end up wanting to look at your chain just when you shouldn't: in heavy traffic, or picking your way up a steep, rocky logging road.

The final reason for having a start-up gear in the left column is related to braking. The 61-38 downshift that you make while coming to a stop is done with your left hand, which allows you to simultaneously apply your rear brake with your right hand. Experienced bicyclists often train themselves to apply their rear brake slightly before their front brake so that, when an emergency stop is required, they are more likely to reach for their rear brake. *Emergency stops using only the front brake can throw the rider head-first over the front of the bicycle.* (Don't use the rear brake alone, however — *both* brakes are needed to stop in the shortest possible distance.)

Using the 38-inch gear in Gearing D as a start-up gear is a feature that could be added to any of the strategies A, B, or C shown for this gearing. The 44-inch gear might also be used frequently as a start-up gear, in conjunction with the 71-inch gear; so also the 32-inch gear in conjunction with the 51-inch gear.

STRATEGIES FOR GEARING E (18-SPEED)

With 18-speed gearings you can have more features than are possible with 15-speed gearings, namely, *dual base gears, two* start-up gears, and a *half-step mini-sequence* in the middle of your primary shift sequence. Gearing E illustrates these possibilities.

E	34	46	50
14	66	89	96
16	57	78	84
19	48	65	71
22	42	57	61
26	35	48	52
34	27	37	40

(1)   The 66- and 40-inch gears in the extreme chain deflections positions are duplicated in the 65- and 42-inch gears, respectively. Other duplications are 35-37, 37-40, 48-48, and 57-57.

(2)   The highest gear is 96 inches, while the lowest is 27 inches.

(3)   All of the vertical changes within each column are half- or full-step changes.

(4)   Places to single-shift between the left and middle columns are at 27-37 or 35-48. Possible single-shifts between the center and right columns are at 48-52, 57-61, 65-71, 78-84, and 89-96.

(5)   One advantage to 18-speed gearings is that it is possible to have *dual base gears,* such as the 57- and 65-inch gears, each using minimum chain deflection. This allows both the 42- and 48-inch gears in the left column to be used frequently as start-up gears.

Gearing E, with one possible primary shift sequence (Dual-option Crossover strategy), two secondary gears, two start-up gears connected to dual base gears, and 57-65-71 half-step mini-sequence, is shown below.

E	34	46	50
14	66	⑧⑨	96
16	57	⑦⑧	84
19	48 — 65		71
22	42 — 57		61
26	35	48	52
34	27	37	40

There are quite a few single-shift primary shifting sequences that could be used with this gearing. The one shown contains as many features as you will find in any strategy: the Single-shift Dual-option Crossover shift strategy in the center and right columns, two secondary gears, and two start-up gears connected to dual base gears. Moreover, the 65-inch base gear is in the middle of the 57-65-71 half-step mini-sequence, which is a nice feature to have in the middle of the primary sequence.

When your route on paved roads takes you through rolling hills, you can make use of the momentum that you gain going downhill to help you get up the next hill, but to do so special shifting techniques are necessary.

Since momentum is mass times velocity, you can maximize your momentum by maximizing your velocity (within limits of safety, of course). So the first step is to gain as much momentum as you can by shifting to your highest 96-inch gear and pedaling while going downhill. When you reach the bottom of the hill you have much momentum, but as soon as you start to go uphill you begin to lose it very fast. You want to shift, while pedaling uphill, in a manner that will enable you to retain as much of your momentum as you can. To do this, plan ahead to shift from your highest gear down to your lowest gear in three or four shifts, such as the 96-71-48-35-27 sequence shown below. (You are losing momentum so fast that you need large changes between gears to be efficient.)

E	34	46	50
14	66	89	(96)
16	57	78	84
19	(48)	65	(71)
22	42	57	61
26	(35)	48	52
34	(27)	37	40

The timing of your shifts as you go uphill is especially important. Downshift to an easier gear too soon, and you lose too much speed and momentum. But if you downshift too late, your legs will not be able to maintain a sufficiently high cadence and there may be too much strain on your chain to allow you to downshift. Pedal in each gear until you feel that the pedaling is *about to become* difficult. Before there is too much strain on the chain or on your knees, shift to the next lower gear. Pedal in that gear for as long as the pedaling is relatively easy, and then downshift again. Continue this until you finally reach the gear that will enable you to get over the hill. Only in the last gear, your lowest, should you do any difficult pedaling.

Learning this "rolling hills" technique is easy. With just a little practice you will find that you are getting a "free" ride quite far uphill, and that only a little bit of difficult pedaling remains. However, because this technique requires going downhill very fast, you need to be certain that it is safe to do so. Other bicyclists ahead of you, unaware of your rapid approach, may weave into your path. Motor vehicles approaching from the rear (you have a mirror, of course) may prohibit you from passing other cyclists. Vehicles ahead of you slowing down to turn (or stopped, waiting to make a left turn) may block your path. And the road surface ahead may not be as smooth as you think it is. (This technique is not recommended for off-pavement riding unless you are very experienced and know the terrain well.) Recognize that the "rolling hills" technique is somewhat risky, and be certain that you will be able to ride in a safe, courteous manner before you start "bombing" downhill.

STRATEGIES FOR GEARING F (18-SPEED MOUNTAIN BIKE)

Gearing F, below, is typical of the type of gearing found on mountain bikes. If you are going to do much off-pavement riding, you will want to use the customary "independent column" strategy (for which this gearing is designed) as shown in Strategy A. If you plan to use this type of gearing mainly for street riding, you might choose Strategy B or C.

F	28	38	48
14	52	71	89
16	46	62	78
19	38	52	66
22	33	45	57
26	28	38	48
30	24	33	42

Gearing F (26-inch wheels)

Off-pavement riding requires a high degree of concentration on road surface and terrain. Holes, bumps, rocks, sticks, sharp turns, and steep uphills and downhills demand your attention, and there isn't much time to think about a complicated shift sequence. Because of this, off-pavement riders tend to use their three columns of gears independently, and do not worry so much about where to cross from one column to another. Strategy A, an example of this, is shown below.

F	28	38	48
14	52	71	89
16	46	62	78
19	38	52	66
22	33	45	57
26	28	38	48
30	24	33	42

Strategy A, Gearing F (26-inch wheels)

The right column is used mainly for riding on pavement. The middle column is used for nearly level unpaved roads, and the 2 or 3 smallest gears in the left column are used for difficult uphill climbs. (Of course, since conditions change so rapidly off-pavement — type of surface, grade, sharp turns — elements of the "start-up gear" and "rolling hills" techniques are also used as necessary.)

Observe that all of the vertical changes within each column are between 4 and 12 gear-inches; there is never a need to change columns to avoid an unpleasantly large shift. Also note that there is much duplication, especially between the left and center columns. This isn't necessarily a bad thing; if you get into the left column to use the 24- or 28-inch gears, and anticipate the need to return to these gears soon, you can stay in the left column and have the same gears you would have in the lower portion of the middle column.

If, however, you are going to use Gearing F mainly for riding on paved roads, you will want to look for a base gear. The 52- and 45-inch gears in the center of the matrix are in the ideal positions for base gears, but are rather small to be used as favorite gears on pavement. You might consider Strategy B, below.

F	28	38	48
14	52	71	89
16	46	62	78
19	38	52	(66)
22	33	45	(57)
26	28	38	48
30	24	33	42

Strategy B, Gearing F (26-inch wheels)

If you like the 62-inch gear as a base gear, you could use the 24-28-38-45-52-62-71-78-89 sequence shown; note the 1-cog double shift at 71-78, and the 46-inch gear as a start-up gear.

If the 66-inch gear appeals to you as a base gear, you could use Strategy C, below.

F	28	38	48
14	52	(71)	89
16	46	(62)	78
19	38	(52)	66
22	33	45	57
26	28	38	48
30	24	33	42

Strategy C, Gearing F (26-inch wheels)

Because Gearing F was designed for off-pavement riding, both of the pavement strategies shown lack the niceties of the strategies for Gearing E. The right column of Gearing F is *adequate* for use on pavement, but if you want a full-featured pavement strategy, you really need another gearing.

Gearing F illustrates that the manner in which you *use* your bicycle is the most important factor when it comes to selecting an appropriate gearing. Other important factors are your physical condition, the terrain on which you ride, your reasons for riding, and your philosophy of shifting. Manufacturers do the best they can in selecting gearings for the bicycles they produce, but because there are so many variables they are unable to please everyone. So if you enjoy bicycling to the extent that it is a significant part of your life, you may wish to add to your pleasure by reading Part II of this book, and selecting a gearing which fits your personal needs.

PART II

SELECTING A NEW GEARING

INTRODUCTION
TO PART II

Having a gearing that suits your own local terrain, physical ability, riding style, and strategies of shifting adds greatly to the physical enjoyment derived from your bicycle as well as improving your performance. But there is also a certain aesthetic satisfaction found in using a gearing which you have chosen personally. Whenever you select features of your bicycle, such as color, saddle style, etc., the bicycle becomes an extension of your personality; so also with its gearing. In short, you like your bicycle more when you know that its gearing contains the features you consider to be important. The best way to obtain such a gearing is to select it yourself!

The recent mountain bike revolution has led to new ideas about the types of gearings suitable for off-pavement use. In response to this, manufacturers have improved both the quality and design of gearing components, which has benefited the *general* bicycling population. So also has the indexed shifting revolution led to new possibilities for increased enjoyment of your bicycle

To choose a new gearing wisely you need to know how the components relate to one another and their limitations (Chapter 6), the different types of gearings found effective by other riders (Chapter 7), and a general process for making your selection (Chapter 8). The appendices provide enough gearings that you should be able to find either exactly what you want, or a gearing close enough to require only slight modification.

6. COMPONENT RELATIONSHIPS AND LIMITATIONS

Many bicyclists reach a point when they wish to consider the possibility of making a change in the gearing on their bicycles. How involved this will be, and how much it will cost, depends upon what gearing is desired and what components are already on the bicycle. Changing gearing is not only a matter of changing chainrings and cogs; sometimes the existing derailleurs and shift levers will accommodate the new gearing and sometimes they will not. (Compatibility is an absolute requirement for indexed systems, of course.) This chapter shows how these components relate to one another, describes their limitations, and provides other information needed when considering a change of gearing.

CHAINRINGS

The pedals of your bicycle are attached to the crankarms. The crankarms are attached to a spindle which goes through the frame. The *bottom bracket assembly* consists of the spindle and those parts used to mount it to the frame, namely bearings, cups, races, and lockring. The chainrings are attached either to the right crankarm, or to the right side of the spindle, just next to the right crankarm.

To be precise, the phrase *chainring set* refers to that collection of parts consisting of the crankarms, chainrings, and any necessary bolts. It does not include the bottom bracket assembly. The word *crankset* traditionally is used ambiguously, sometimes meaning exactly the same as chainring set, but at other times meaning the chainring set along with the bottom bracket assembly.

For many years only a very few bicyclists, usually racers, changed the gearings on their bicycles. Consequently, in order to keep prices down, manufacturers equipped bikes with cranksets not designed to facilitate changing chainrings. For these types of cranksets, either new chainrings are unavailable or the old chainrings are not detachable from other parts of the crankset. If you have one of these types of cranksets it may be necessary to replace it with one of the detachable type in order to obtain your desired gearing.

DETACHABLE CHAINRING SET

In this type of chainring set, the chainrings, left and right crankarms, and spindle are all separate pieces (Figure 6). The right crankarm along with five "spider legs" are molded (cast) from the same piece of metal. The chainrings are separate and bolted to the spider legs. Because the chainrings are so easily detachable from the rest of the crankset, they are fairly inexpensive and easy to change; simply purchase new chainrings and bolt them in place of the old ones. Almost all triple chainring sets are of the detachable type.

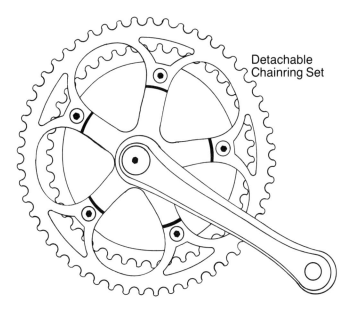

Detachable
Chainring Set

Figure 6

The bolts that attach the chainrings to the spider legs are arranged in a circle. In fact, some triple cranksets use two bolt circles, one for the middle and outer chainrings and another for the inner chainring. But various manufacturers often use different-size circles, and so chainrings from one brand or model may not be interchangeable with those of another. Manufacturers and catalogs specify the size of bolt circles by listing *bolt circle diameters* which, on most detachable chainring sets, are 74mm, 110mm, 130mm and 133mm. Measure from the center of the spindle to the center of one of the bolts to find the *radius* of the bolt circle; then multiply by 2 to get the diameter.

PURCHASING A NEW CHAINRING SET

When purchasing a detachable chainring set, it is wise to consider not only the gearing that is presently desired, but also possible future changes. Not all manufacturers provide every size chainring (number of teeth) for their various models. Popular models provide a full range of chainrings, and replacements are likely to be available when another change of gearing is considered. Your dealer can provide information concerning popular brands of chainring sets.

Each model of detachable chainring set is available with crankarms of two or three different lengths, usually 170mm, 172.5mm, or 175mm, and you will have to choose the length you want when purchasing this type of crankset. Short crankarms permit a slightly higher cadence whereas long crankarms provide slightly more leverage. If you don't know what size to choose, but feel comfortable with the crankarms you now have, then stay with that size. You can determine the length of your present crankarms by measuring from the center of the spindle to the center of the threaded hole which accepts the pedal.

The new chainring set that you purchase must be compatible with the bottom bracket assembly to which it will be attached. Not all chainring sets will fit onto all spindles. You may need to take your bicycle to a dealer or mechanic to determine the brand and model of your present bottom bracket assembly. At the same time, your dealer should be able to tell you which cranksets it will accept. (One other caution: if your bicycle has an *indexed* front derailleur, be sure to install *steel* chainrings — aluminum is not sturdy enough for the forced shifts.)

If you choose to purchase a new bottom bracket assembly you will need to know whether you have English, Italian, French, Swiss, or Whitworth threading in the bottom bracket of your bicycle because parts of the assembly screw into the frame. The easiest way to determine which threading is on your bicycle is to ask a dealer or mechanic; very often they can tell just by knowing who manufactured your frame. Frames made in the United States and Japan usually have English threading.

Do not be disheartened about changing gearing. Changing chainrings *may* involve replacing both the chainring set and the bottom bracket assembly, but it also may not. In fact, it is sometimes possible to convert a double crankset to a triple by purchasing and installing only the third chainring, a slightly longer spindle and some new bolts.

OVAL CHAINRINGS

Oval (elliptical, or out-of-round) chainrings are designed to accommodate the fact that your legs provide a different amount of power, and a slightly different cadence, during the first portion of each downstroke than during the latter portion. Theoretically, oval chainrings produce less side-to-side sway and a more efficient use of power. Even though they are currently standard equipment on production-line mountain bikes, their overall effectiveness is somewhat controversial among competitive cyclists.

All oval chainring sets are of the detachable type, and it is usually possible to purchase just the chainrings. So if you have round detachable chainrings with the correct bolt circle diameter(s), you can replace them with oval chainrings if you wish. The shape of the chainrings you use has *no* effect on your gear-inch numbers, but oval chainrings *do* affect the capacity of your front derailleur in a manner that will be discussed later in this chapter.

FRONT DERAILLEURS

Whenever a change of chainrings is being considered it is also necessary to think about the front derailleur that will be used. If you have a double crankset, you need only worry about *front derailleur capacity*; but if you have a triple crankset you may need a new *large capacity front derailleur* to enable your new gearing to shift properly.

FRONT DERAILLEUR CAPACITY

Front derailleur capacity is measured in number of teeth (T) and represents the largest change that the front derailleur can make in shifting between the smallest and largest chainrings. For example, a front derailleur with a capacity of 18T can make the shift from a smallest 34T (round) chainring to a largest 52T (round) chainring (52-34=18), or from 36T to 52T (52-36=16), but is not designed to shift from 32T to 52T (52-32=20). (How oval chainrings affect front derailleur capacity is discussed below.)

Suppose your bicycle has a double crankset with 40T and 52T (round) chainrings. The front derailleur has a capacity of at least 12T, but possibly not much more. If a change to a triple crankset with 26T, 45T, and 50T chainrings is being considered, a new front derailleur of capacity 24T (50-26=24) will probably be required.

The exact manner in which oval chainrings affect front derailleur capacity is not yet known, primarily because the optimum shape of oval chainrings is still being determined. (Recent versions of oval chainrings are more round than their earlier counterparts.)

The leading manufacturer of oval chainrings, who does not recommend mixing oval and round chainrings on the same crankset, indicates that the capacity of a front derailleur should be considered 4T smaller when used with oval chainrings rather than with round ones. For example, this same manufacturer lists one of its front derailleurs as having a *round capacity* of 26T but an *oval capacity* of only 22T. However, some riders have found that little (or no) change in front derailleur capacity occurs when "all-oval" chainrings are used. This book recommends that you follow your manufacturer's advice if available. Otherwise, to be safe, subtract 4T from the round capacity of a front derailleur to obtain its oval capacity, especially when purchasing components from a catalog. (If only one capacity is listed, assume that it is for round chainrings.) If you are buying from a dealer, make sure the dealer knows that you plan to use oval chainrings and guarantees that the front derailleur you purchase will work.

When mixing oval and round chainrings on the same crankset, as many riders successfully do, it is convenient to think in terms of how much round front derailleur capacity *your gearing needs*. If the oval chainring is the largest (with, say, 52T), think of it as a round chainring 2T larger (54T). Then subtract the number of teeth on the smallest chainring (say 40T) to get the round front derailleur capacity you need (54T - 40T = 14T). If the oval chainring is the smallest it will be safest to think of it as a round chainring with the same number of teeth, and compute the round capacity you need merely by subtracting from the number of teeth on the largest chainring.

LARGE CAPACITY FRONT DERAILLEURS

By a *large capacity front derailleur,* this book will mean any front derailleur having capacity (for round chainrings) of 22T or more. Typically these derailleurs are used with 15- and 18-speed gearings selected for touring or off-pavement use.

Large capacity front derailleurs vary in their design according to the difference between the number of teeth on the *middle* and *outer* chainrings of the cranksets for which they are to be used.

As this is being written, several designs exist. Each is intended for a particular range of middle- to-outer-ring difference. The important thing is to know that they are available for 15- and 18-speed gearings, and that each design works best for a particular range. Check the latest magazines and catalogs, or confer with a knowledgeable bicycle mechanic, to choose a large capacity front derailleur that will work best for your gearing.

COGS

The cogs and the spacers are attached to the freewheel (Figure 7). Individual cogs can be changed, provided the freewheel manufacturer makes them with the number of teeth you want. Cogs ranging in size from 13T to 34T are fairly easy to obtain, and it is best to stay within this range. By carefully selecting the model of freewheel, you might be able to get cogs of 11T, 12T, 36T or 38T, but using these cogs can lead to derailleur or chain problems. It will be least expensive to limit your selection of cogs to those available for the freewheel you already have.

USING YOUR PRESENT FREEWHEEL

On some bicycles the freewheel is built into the hub of the rear wheel. With this type of arrangement, unless you are willing to replace your rear wheel, you will need to limit your selection of cogs to those provided by the manufacturer of your hub.

On most bicycles the freewheel can be replaced easily — it just screws onto the hub. But there is no point in changing freewheels if you are satisfied with the one you have and are able to obtain the few new cogs that you need.

Freewheel, Exploded View

Figure 7

71

(If you want to change many cogs, it may be more economical to purchase a whole new freewheel, even if it is the same basic model as your present freewheel.)

If you have an indexed shifting system, you will probably have to limit your selection of cogs to those available for the freewheels which are compatible with your system. In some cases your present freewheel may be the only one possible. Your dealer should be able to tell you which freewheels and cogs to consider.

REPLACING INDIVIDUAL COGS

Special tools are required to loosen and remove the first few cogs from the freewheel, but many shops charge only a small amount to do this for you so that you can replace and clean cogs yourself. If you do this, be aware that many cogs are designed with an outside face and an inside face, and will not work properly if reversed. Carefully examine each cog to detect the difference between the faces; the type of face that is *inside* on one cog may be the *outside* of another. Therefore it is best to make a small scratch on the inside face of each cog as it is removed. This is highly recommended, as you will probably want to clean your cogs before you reassemble them.

When removing the cogs and spacers from the freewheel, carefully place them on your workbench in the order in which they were removed. Some adjacent cogs may have two spacers between them whereas others have only one. Care must be taken to reassemble them in the proper order.

Replacement cogs should be installed in a manner similar to those they replace. For instance, if you are changing a 13-15-17-19-24-30T freewheel to one of 13-15-17-19-25-32T, install the 25T cog with the same type of inside face that the 24T cog had on the inside; so also with the 32T and 30T cogs. If your chain won't shift onto a certain cog from a particular direction, most likely that cog needs to be reversed.

If your chain begins to "skip" when you are using some new cogs, you will need a new chain. This is because chains and cogs tend to wear out together. But try the old chain with the new cogs; sometimes they work together just fine.

SELECTING A NEW FREEWHEEL

To obtain the gearing you want it may be necessary to choose a new freewheel. To determine the cogs available for different freewheels, you may need to ask your dealer to let you look through manufacturer's catalogs (be prepared to take some notes).

Don't feel limited by the "stock" freewheels you see listed in mail-order catalogs or magazines. Decide upon the cogs *you* want, and look for a model of freewheel that provides those cogs; if you stay within the 13T-34T range, you should be able to get exactly what you want. Your dealer may have to order some of the cogs, but he should be willing to do so; if not, find another dealer.

Some freewheels make less noise than others, but this is not necessarily an indication of superior quality; some excellent freewheels are fairly noisy. If you ride frequently you will want to have a popular freewheel so you can obtain replacement cogs easily; the cogs used most wear out faster than the others.

Another concern when changing freewheels is the space provided for the freewheel on the frame of your bicycle. The rear wheel is attached to the frame in slots or holes called *rear dropouts*. On some bicycles the distance between the *inside* faces of the rear dropouts is 120-122mm; on other bicycles it is 126mm or 130mm.

Bicycles with 120-122mm rear dropouts can accept either a *standard 5-cog* or an *ultra* (narrow) *6-cog freewheel*. These two types of freewheels are both approximately the same width and require the same amount of space. The ultra 6-cog freewheel puts 6 cogs in the place of 5 by using thinner spacers between the cogs. This in turn requires the use of a narrow chain. Bicycles with 126mm rear dropouts can accept either a *standard 6-cog* or an *ultra 7-cog* freewheel.

Whenever you change freewheels you should investigate which chain to use with your new freewheel. Some chains work especially well with certain freewheels but perform poorly with others. You can follow the freewheel manufacturer's recommendation about which chain to use, ask a qualified mechanic, or read various magazine articles which deal with this topic. Ultra freewheels require the use of a narrow chain; with standard freewheels you can use either a narrow or wide chain.

REAR DERAILLEUR CAPACITIES

The first item of concern when choosing a rear derailleur is its *largest-cog capacity*. This number is a measure (in number of teeth) of the largest cog onto which the derailleur is capable of shifting the chain. A freewheel with 14-17-20-24-28-34T cogs requires a rear dearailleur with a largest-cog capacity of 34T or more. Rear derailleurs whose largest-cog capacities range up to 32T are easy to obtain, although others can be found with capacities of 34T and 36T.

The other item of concern when selecting a rear derailleur is its capacity to deal with excess chain, as certain gears require the use of less chain than do others. For instance, less chain is required to go around a 28T chainring and a 20T cog than around a 48T chainring and a 20T cog. The rear derailleur provides a path for any excess chain and is said to *wrap up* the excess.

The *wrap-up capacity* (also called *maximum total capacity, total capacity,* or just *capacity*) of a rear derailleur is a measure of the *largest* amount of excess chain that the derailleur can wrap up. Wrap-up capacities range from about 22T to 42T, although the 42T capacity is found on only one model.

WRAP-UP REQUIRED BY A GEARING

Each gearing itself also produces a variable amount of excess chain. The maximum amount of excess chain produced by a gearing is called its *required wrap-up* (measured in number of teeth). This number is calculated by adding the difference between the largest and smallest chainrings to the difference between the largest and smallest cogs.

The required wrap-up of Gearing A is shown below.

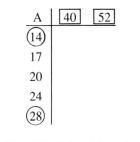

$$(52 - 40) + (28 - 14) = 12 + 14 = 26T.$$

This gearing requires a rear derailleur with a wrap-up capacity of at least 26T, and a largest-cog capacity of at least 28T.

The required wrap-up of Gearing F is shown below.

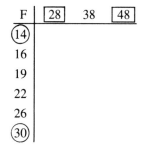

$$(48 - 28) + (30 - 14) = 36T.$$

This gearing requires a rear derailleur which can wrap up 36T of excess chain and shift the chain onto a 30T largest cog.

Rear derailleurs with large wrap-up capacities have longer cages than those with smaller capacities, and usually do not shift quite as quickly. The best performance is obtained by using a rear derailleur whose capacities are reasonably close to those required by the gearing. For example, any rear derailleur appropriate for Gearing F will also work on Gearing A, but not as well as one whose capacities are closer to those required by Gearing A.

EXCEEDING REAR DERAILLEUR WRAP-UP CAPACITY

If you stay within the 13T - 34T cog range recommended earlier, the only way to have both a 100-inch highest gear and a 19-inch or 20-inch lowest gear is to use a gearing which requires more wrap-up than any existing rear derailleur can provide. Gearing G, which requires 43T of derailleur wrap-up, is typical of such a gearing.

G	24	39	48
13	50	81	100
15	43	70	86
17	38	62	76
19	34	55	68
25	26	42	52
32	20	33	41

Riders who use gearings such as these sacrifice the use of some gears in order to do so. Exactly which gears must be avoided depends upon whether they have chosen to use more chain or less chain than is normally required. *Both methods present an element of danger if an attempt is made to shift into those gears which should be avoided.*

THE LONG-CHAIN METHOD

The *long-chain method* of using a gearing which requires more wrap-up than the rear derailleur can provide requires the use of enough chain to connect the largest chainring to the largest cog. This is the *maximum chain gear,* since it uses more chain than any other gear, and is located in the lower right corner of the matrix. Even though you do not intend to use the maximum chain gear because of extreme chain deflection (besides, it is probably duplicated elsewhere in the matrix), with the long-chain method nothing should go wrong if it is used inadvertently.

However, there will be too much excess chain for the derailleur to wrap up when some of the gears requiring the smallest amounts of chain are used. These are the gears in the upper left corner of the matrix, in which the smallest chainring is connected to the one, two, or three smallest cogs. When these gears are used inadvertently, *usually* the excess chain just hangs low and no harm is done. *But it is possible for the use of these gears, especially as start-up gears, to cause the chain to jump off one of the pulleys and "jam up" the rear derailleur. This results in a bent rear derailleur, a "frozen" rear wheel, and possibly a serious accident.*

Suppose that you choose the long-chain method of using Gearing G (43T required wrap-up) with a rear derailleur having a 39T or 40T wrap-up capacity. You will need to use enough links so that the chain will shift onto the 41-inch maximum chain gear. Even though you do not intend to use this gear, it will be safe to do so inadvertently.

But now it will happen that there is too much chain for the rear derailleur to wrap up when the 50-inch, 43-inch, and possibly 38-inch gears are used. These are the gears which use the least amounts of chain and leave the most to be wrapped up. *Attempts to use these gears, especially as start-up gears, can cause your rear wheel to "lock up" and leave you in an extremely dangerous position!*

When first installing a gearing/derailleur/chain combination such as this, you will need to test carefully the gears in the left column to see which ones can be used. Do this *with your bicycle on a repair stand.* Shift into the gear in the lower left corner of your matrix (smallest chainring, largest cog). With your rear derailleur, one cog at a time, *slowly* shift the chain onto successively smaller cogs (you are shifting up the left column of your matrix). Watch your chain and rear derailleur carefully to see how they behave in these gears, especially the ones which produce more excess chain than the derailleur can wrap up. Most likely the excess chain will just hang low and no harm will be done, *but if the chain jumps out of either of the pulleys in the derailleur, or if any part of the derailleur gets caught in the cogs, STOP!* —*you will be unable to use any gear in which this happens.*

You will also need to test the start-up capability of any gear in the left column which appears safe for use in the above test. With your bicycle still on the repair stand, shift into a potential start-up gear, stop the rear wheel with your brake, and then begin to "pedal." If the chain jumps off the jockey wheels, or if the derailleur gets caught in the cogs, you will be unable to use this gear as a start-up gear.

Finally, *repeat the above tests while actually riding your bicycle in a safe location.* It is especially important that you *slowly* re-test each of the potential start-up gears. These gears can appear safe when the bicycle is on a repair stand, but fail (and possibly cause an accident) under actual riding conditions. If the long-chain method turns out to be inappropriate for your needs, you can consider trying the short-chain method.

THE SHORT-CHAIN METHOD

Note: Before actually using the short-chain method you MUST apply the chain-shortening tests described in Appendix K.

The short-chain method of exceeding the wrap-up capacity of the rear derailleur usually requires a chain which is just two fewer links than the long-chain method. With the short-chain method you use no more chain than the derailleur can wrap up when the bicycle is in the *minimum chain gear,* the one in the upper left corner of your matrix, the one in which the chain connects the smallest chainring to the smallest cog. Since this is the gear which produces the most excess chain, and the derailleur is able to wrap it all up, there is never more excess chain than the rear derailleur can handle. *All* of the gears in the *left* column can be used safely.

But now there will not be enough chain to enable you to shift into the maximum chain gear, and perhaps some others which use large amounts of chain. You will need to apply the chain-shortening tests found in Appendix K to see how your derailleurs cope with the shorter chain, and to determine which gears are safe for use.

If you choose the short-chain method of using Gearing G (43T required wrap-up) with a rear derailleur having a wrap-up capacity of 39T or 40T, begin with as much chain as your rear derailleur is able to wrap up when you are in the 50-inch gear, but *no more chain than this.* This will enable you to use the 50-inch gear and all the others in the left column. But most likely there will not be enough chain to enable you to shift into the 41-inch gear, and you will need to apply the chain-shortening tests in Appendix K to see if it is safe for you to use this arrangement.

A NEW GEARING OR A NEW BICYCLE?

If your new gearing is going to be expensive, think about whether you want a new gearing or a new bicycle. If you are dissatisfied with other features of your bicycle, and expect to replace it sometime in the future, then do so now and save most of the cost of a new gearing. If negotiated at the time of purchase, so that changes can be made at the time of assembly, many dealers will replace unwanted components (both gearing and non-gearing) with more desirable ones and charge only for the added value. But if you wait until the bicycle is used, you will probably have to pay full price for the new components as well as an installation charge.

7. TYPES OF GEARINGS

There are four basic types of 10- and 12-speed gearings: Half-step, Alpine, Wide-step, and Crossover. Triple cranksets have led to 15- and 18-speed gearings called Half-step + Granny, Alpine + Granny, and Double Crossover. This chapter describes each of these types of gearings and discusses their advantages and disadvantages, but first some special terminology is necessary.

SPECIAL TERMINOLOGY

At times it is necessary to discuss the gears, and their positions in the matrix, without reference to any specific gearing. The standard way of doing this (for 10-speeds) is to use the generic chart shown below, where L is the lower (smaller) chainring, H is the higher (larger) chainring, and 5, 4, 3, 2, and 1 represent the cogs. H5 is the highest gear on the bicycle and L1 the lowest; this is consistent with the gear-inch matrices seen previously.

	L	H
5	L5	H5
4	L4	H4
3	L3	H3
2	L2	H2
1	L1	H1

For 18-speed gearings the chart shown below is used, where M represents the middle chainring. H6 is the highest gear, L1 the lowest.

	L	M	H
6	L6	M6	H6
5	L5	M5	H5
4	L4	M4	H4
3	L3	M3	H3
2	L2	M2	H2
1	L1	M1	H1

Traditionally the phrase *Granny gear* refers to a very low gear, but there is no standard agreement concerning the size of Granny gears. This book will call any gear that is 27 gear-inches or lower a Granny gear.

The *range* of a gearing refers to the difference between its highest and lowest gears. A *wide-range* gearing might have a 25-inch lowest gear and a 100-inch top gear, a *medium-range* gearing might span 40- to 100-inch, and a *narrow-range* gearing 55- to 100-inch, although there are no definite cut-off points which define these terms exactly.

HALF-STEP GEARINGS

In a *Half-step gearing* the cogs and chainrings are chosen so that the *percent* of change when shifting from one cog to the next remains approximately constant, and the percent of change between chainrings is approximately half that between cogs. (Chainrings differing by 4-6T are frequently used in this type of gearing.) The percents are usually calculated by dividing the larger number of teeth by the smaller, and disregarding the 1 at the left of the decimal point. For instance, when shifting between a 17T cog and a 14T cog, divide 17 by 14 to get 1.21. This means that, with the same chainring, the gear using the 14T cog is 121% of (or 21% higher than) the gear using the 17T cog.

For the Half-step Gearing H, below, 17/14 = 1.21 (a 21% change), 21/17 = 1.24 (a 24% change), 26/21 = 1.24 (another 24% change), 32/26 = 1.23 (a 23% change), and 52/47 = 1.11 (an 11% change). The 21%, 24%, 24%, and 23% freewheel changes are approximately the same number, and the 11% chainring change is approximately half that number.

H	47	52
14	91	100
17	75	83
21	60	67
26	49	54
32	40	44

In Half-step gearings, single-shifts with the front derailleur result in approximately half as much change as single-shifts with the rear derailleur. In Gearing H, for instance, the 60-67 front derailleur single-shift produces approximately half as much change as the 60-75 rear derailleur single-shift. But the *Half-step shift sequence,* which many riders use with this type of gearing, contains no single-shifts with the rear derailleur. (A shift sequence is usually part of an overall shift strategy, although it can be the entire strategy.)

HALF-STEP SHIFT SEQUENCE

The 10-speed *Half-step shift sequence* shown below is L1-H1-L2-H2-L3-H3-L4-H4-L5-H5 (-L6-H6 for 12-speeds). It begins with the smallest gear and zig-zags its way up the matrix, as shown. When used with a Half-step gearing, it takes you *in order* from the smallest gear to the largest with consecutive changes which feel similar to one another. Single-shifts alternate with 1-cog double-shifts.

	L	H
5	L5 ⌐ H5
4	L4 ⟍ H4
3	L3 ⌐ H3
2	L2 ⟍ H2
1	L1 ⟍ H1

The slight, but relatively even, changes produced as you shift a Half-step gearing with a Half-step shift sequence permit you always to be in the right gear, the one which provides the best balance between the use of your cardiovascular system and the strength in your legs, and is the major advantage of this type of gearing. The other advantage is the lack of duplications. The disadvantages are the double-shifts, along with a lowest gear that isn't very low, although many riders prefer this type of gearing.

When Gearing H is used with the Half-step shift sequence, the resulting changes are 4 gear-inches (40-44), 5 inches (44-49 and 49-54), 6 inches (54-60), 7 inches (60-67), 8 inches (67-75, 75-83, and 83-91), and 9 inches (91-100).

H	47	52
14	91	100
17	75	83
21	60	67
26	49	54
32	40	44

All but the 9-inch change are half-steps of change, as defined in Chapter 5. The lowest gear is 40 inches, but this could be lowered by changing to a 34T cog and 45T and 50T chainrings, as in the next example.

Even though the freewheel percentage changes of 21%, 24%, 24%, and 31% in Gearing I (below) are not so nearly equal to one another as they were in Gearing H, Gearing I is still regarded as a Half-step gearing.

I	45	50
14	87	96
17	72	79
21	58	64
26	47	52
34	36	40

The 5T chainring difference produces the same 11% change as it does in Gearing H. (Actually 52/47 = 1.106 whereas 50/45 = 1.111.) If you are seeking a Half-step gearing to suit your particular needs, it helps to remember that pairs of chainrings having the same *difference* in number of teeth produce about the same percentage change. Many other 10- and 12-speed Half-step gearings are identified in the appendices using the symbol HS.

7. TYPES OF GEARINGS

HALF-STEP + GRANNY GEARINGS

Any 15- or 18-speed gearing in which the middle and outer chainrings form a Half-step gearing and the inner chainring provides one or two Granny gears is called a *Half-step + Granny* gearing. Tourists, and others who have need of a wide range of gears, often choose this type of gearing as it has all the advantages of a Half-step gearing while also providing low gears. If you require an especially low (e.g., 19-inch) gear, the required wrap-up of such a gearing may be quite large, as in Gearing J, below.

J	24	45	50
14	(46)	87 — 96	
17	(38)?	72 — 79	
21	30	58 — 64	
26	25	47 — 52	
34	19	36 — 40	

A 24T chainring added to Gearing I produces a wide-range Half-step + Granny gearing; Gearing J is an example. As often happens in Half-step + Granny gearings, there is a 2-cog double-shift between the small and middle chainrings when shifting through the gears in strict order.

The required wrap-up of Gearing J is 46T, which exceeds the wrap-up capacity of all current rear derailleurs. If you wish to make occasional use of the 40-inch gear in the extreme chain deflection position, as indicated in the sequence above, you will need to install this gearing with the long-chain method and test accordingly for safety. (Note that the top one or two gears in the left column may not be safe to use. See pages 76 and 77 for an explanation of the dangers.)

If you prefer the short-chain method of exceeding the rear derailleur wrap-up capacity, you could shift Gearing J as shown below. (In this case, you will probably not be able to shift into the gears in the lower right corner of the matrix, as shown. See Appendix K.)

J	24	45	50
14	46	87 — 96	
17	38	72 — 79	
21	30	58 — 64	
26	25	47 — 52	
34	19	(36)?	(40)

If you wish to avoid exceeding the rear derailleur wrap-up capacity altogether, you could use a 28-45-50T crankset with a 14-17-21-26-32T freewheel; this would require 40T of derailleur wrap-up, and provide a 24-inch Granny gear. Other 15- and 18-speed Half-step + Granny gearings are provided in the appendices and labeled as HS+G.

ALPINE GEARINGS

Alpine gearings are sometimes referred to as one-and-a-half-step gearings. Like in Half-step gearings, the freewheel percentage changes must be approximately equal to each other, but the percent of chainring change must be approximately one-and-a-half (instead of just one-half) times the freewheel change. (Chainrings differing by 10-14T are frequently used in this type of gearing.) This produces a wider range gearing than a Half-Step gearing with the same freewheel, maintains the advantage of having no duplications, but also produces a large gap between the largest and next-to-largest gears.

The most common Alpine gearing is the 10-speed Gearing A, seen in earlier chapters.

A	40	52
14	77	100
17	64	83
20	54	70
24	45	59
28	39	50

The freewheel percentage changes are 21%, 17%, 20%, and 17%. The chainring change of 30% is approximately one-and-a-half times the freewheel change. It ranges from 39 gear-inches to 100 inches with no duplications, but the 83-100 gap is larger than desirable. Unfortunately this, and all Alpine gearings, are difficult to shift when the *Alpine shift sequence* is used.

ALPINE SHIFT SEQUENCE

The 10-speed Alpine shift sequence is L1-L2-H1-L3-H2-L4-H3-L5-H4-H5 (H4-L6-H5-H6 for 12-speeds).

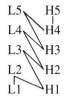

It contains two single-shifts, four 1-cog double-shifts, three 2-cog double-shifts and, when used with an Alpine gearing, takes you sequentially from the lowest to the highest gears. But the double-shifts are so cumbersome that few riders use the Alpine shift sequence with an Alpine (or any) type of gearing.

Because the Alpine shift sequence is so difficult to learn and to perform, seven other strategies, many with a Crossover shift sequence, were illustrated and recommended for Gearing A in Chapter 5. Alpine gearings are not especially poor gearings — they just shouldn't be shifted with the Alpine shift sequence. Other 10- and 12-speed Alpine gearings are listed in the appendices and identified by the letter A.

ALPINE + GRANNY GEARINGS

Any 15- or 18-speed gearing in which the middle and outer chainrings produce an Alpine gearing, and the inner chainring provides at least one Granny gear, is called an *Alpine + Granny* gearing. Because of the shifting problems discussed above, Alpine + Granny gearings are not usually selected for riding on pavement. But the 10-14T difference in chainring teeth often makes these gearings suitable for off-pavement use.

Gearing F, below, is an 18-speed Alpine + Granny gearing. The freewheel changes are 14%, 19%, 16%, 18%, and 15%, and the 38T-48T chainring change is 26%. The 28T chainring produces the 24-inch Granny gear. This gearing, which was discussed in Chapter 5, is typical of those found on mountain bikes and is suitable for off-pavement use when the columns are used independently. Other 15- and 18-speed Alpine + Granny gearings may be found in the appendices by looking for the symbol A+G.

F	28	38	48
14	52	71	89
16	46	62	78
19	38	52	66
22	33	45	57
26	28	38	48
30	24	33	42

Gearing F (26" Wheels)

WIDE-STEP GEARINGS

This book will consider a *Wide-step gearing* to be any 10- or 12-speed non-Alpine gearing in which the larger chainring contains *at least* 14 teeth *more* than the smaller chainring.

Gearing K, below, is an example of a 12-speed Wide-step gearing. The large chainring difference (52 - 34T) is used to produce a wide-range gearing (27-100 inches) on a bicycle with a double crankset, and is the only advantage to this type of gearing. The disadvantage is the large gap between the two columns which necessitates a 2-cog double-shift right in the middle of the shift sequence.

K	34	52
14	66	100
16	57	88
18	51	78
21	44	67
26	35	54
34	27	41

Now that the technology for 15- and 18-speed gearings is so reliable, available, and reasonably priced, there is no longer much need for Wide-step gearings; with a triple crankset you can have a wide-range gearing as well as easy shifting. But for those cyclists who prefer this type of gearing, others are identified in the appendices with the symbol WS.

CROSSOVER GEARINGS

A *Crossover gearing* is any 10- or 12-speed gearing, which is not Half-step, Alpine, or Wide-step, and which is designed to be used with one of the *Single-shift Crossover shift sequences*. Riders who place a high priority on shifting convenience, and who insist upon having a single-shift primary sequence, look for gearings which shift well with one of these sequences. Crossover gearings are designed to do so, but it will be seen that many Half-step gearings also shift well with Crossover shift sequences.

CROSSOVER SHIFT SEQUENCES

The 10-speed Single-shift Crossover shift sequence is L1-L2-L3-H3-H4-H5; the crossover between the two chainrings is made at the middle cog, L3-H3. The other gears (L5, L4, H2, H1) may be totally ignored or used as secondary gears. See below.

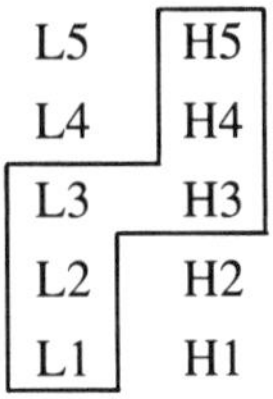

```
L5    H5
L4    H4
L3    H3
L2    H2
L1    H1
```

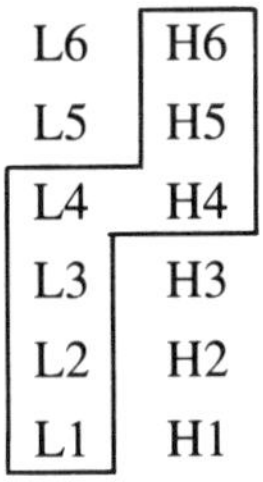

The two possible 12-speed Single-shift Crossover shift sequences are shown below. The crossover between chainrings is made at one of the two center cogs, at either L3-H3 or L4-H4. Gears not in the sequence either may be ignored or used as secondary gears.

```
L6    H6        L6    H6
L5    H5        L5    H5
L4    H4        L4    H4
L3    H3        L3    H3
L2    H2        L2    H2
L1    H1        L1    H1
```

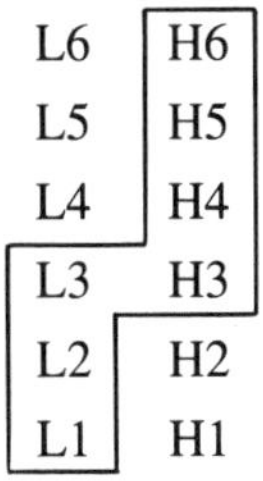

For 12-speed gearings a *Dual-option Crossover shift sequence,* below, is possible, which merely delays the decision about whether to cross over at L3-H3 or L4-H4; the decision is made while riding, as conditions dictate. This strategy uses 8 of the 12 gears on a 12-speed bicycle and is a particularly nice single-shift strategy.

```
L6    H6
L5    H5
L4    H4
L3    H3
L2    H2
L1    H1
```

The traditional 10-speed (double-shift) Crossover shift strategy below is to stay in one column until you run out of gears, and then cross over to the other column, usually with a double-shift, at either L5-H4 or H1-L2. You shift up the left column until you need gears higher than L5, then cross over to the appropriate gear in the right column. Once in the right column, you stay there until you need gears lower than H1, and then cross over to whichever gear you need in the left column. For 12-speeds everything is the same except that the crossover to the right column usually is made at L6-H5 (or L5-H4 if you prefer to avoid the L6 chain-deflection gear). This method of shifting will be referred to as the *traditional Double-shift Crossover strategy.*

```
L5    H5         L5    H5
L4    H4         L4    H4
L3    H3         L3    H3
L2    H2         L2    H2
L1    H1         L1    H1
```

(Shifting up)   (Shifting down)

Even though the traditional Double-shift Crossover strategy is effective, this book purposely emphasizes the Single-shift Crossover sequences because of the large number of recreational riders who seek single-shift strategies. For these riders, the Dual-option Crossover strategy is recommended highly.

CROSSOVER SHIFT SEQUENCES APPLIED TO CROSSOVER GEARINGS

Gearing L, below, is a 10-speed Crossover gearing because it is not Half-step, Alpine, or Wide-step, and the Single-shift Crossover sequence is an effective strategy for this gearing.

L	42	52
14	81	100
16	71	88
19	60	74
24	47	59
32	35	44

Gearing M, below, is a 12-speed Crossover gearing because it is not Half-step, Alpine, or Wide-step, and is well-suited for use with a Single-shift Crossover shift sequence. When used with the Dual-option Crossover sequence as shown, decisions about whether to shift 57-64-76 or 57-68-76 are made while riding, depending upon whether the 64- or 68-inch gear seems more appropriate.

M	40	48
13	83	100
15	(72)	86
17	64	76
19	57	68
25	43	(52)
34	32	41

Gearing N, below, is technically a Crossover gearing because the chainring change of 9% and the freewheel changes of 15%, 13%, 18%, 25%, and 36% do not allow this to be a Half-step gearing.

N	44	48
13	91	100
15	79	86
17	70	76
20	59	65
25	48	52
34	35	38

But if the twelve gears were shifted *in order* from lowest to highest, the zig-zag Half-step shift sequence would be followed. Crossover gearings such as this are identified in the appendices as C(HS). Crossover gearings in which the sequence from lowest to highest follows the Alpine shift sequence (but which are not Alpine gearings because of the percentages), are identified as C(A). All other Crossover gearings are identified as C.

CROSSOVER SHIFT SEQUENCES APPLIED TO OTHER GEAR-INGS

Any gearing may be shifted in any convenient manner. If you prefer a single-shift strategy, do not overlook Half-step or Alpine gearings (especially 12-speeds) as many shift quite well with a Single-shift Crossover sequence.

Gearing O, below, is a legitimate Half-step gearing and could be used effectively with the zig-zag Half-step shift sequence. But it would also shift nicely with the Dual-option Crossover strategy, as shown.

O	46	50
14	89	96
16	78	84
19	65	71
22	57	61
26	48	52
30	41	45

Chapter 5 also showed three Crossover sequences as effective strategies for Gearing C (although it was not identified as an Alpine gearing in that chapter).

DOUBLE CROSSOVER GEARINGS

A *Double Crossover* gearing is any 15- or 18-speed gearing in which the middle and outer chainrings produce a Crossover gearing; the inner chainring usually adds one or two Granny gears. This could just as well be called a Crossover + Granny gearing, but the term Double Crossover is more common, even though there may be a 1-cog double-shift between the inner and middle chainrings.

Double Crossover gearings are popular with riders who prefer a single-shift strategy and who need a wide range of gears for use on pavement, such as tourists who usually choose either this type of gearing or a Half-step + Granny gearing. Assuming that you like a single-shift strategy, the only disadvantage of a Double Crossover gearing is the same as on any gearing with a 20- to 100-inch range: it requires more than 40T of rear derailleur wrap-up.

The addition of a 24T chainring to the Crossover Gearing M produces the 18-speed Double Crossover Gearing P, below.

P	24	40	48
13	50	83	100
15	43	(72)	86
17	38	64	76
19	34	57	68
25	26	43	(52)
34	19	32	41

In effect, this adds only the two extra 19-inch and 26-inch Granny gears, and a 1-cog double-shift at 26-32 (which could be by-passed whenever you choose to single-shift 19-32). Since Gearing P requires 45T of derailleur wrap-up, use of either the long-chain or the short-chain method of exceeding the rear derailleur wrap-up capacity is necessary. Assuming that a rear derailleur with a 40T wrap-up capacity is used, the long-chain method prohibits the 50-, 43-, and probably the 38-inch gear from being used; with the short-chain method only the 41-inch gear cannot be used (see Gearing G in Chapter 5).

Gearing Q, below, is produced by adding a third chainring to the C(HS) Gearing N. Gearings such as this are identified in the appendices as DC(HS). Gearings obtained by adding a third chainring to a C(A) gearing are identified as DC(A). All other Double Crossover gearings are identified with the symbol DC.

Q	26	44	48
13	54	91	100
15	47	79	86
17	41	70	76
20	35	59	65
25	28	48	52
34	21	35	38

8. SELECTING A GEARING

Selecting a new gearing is usually a very rewarding experience, but it can be somewhat complex and time-consuming. This chapter identifies the tasks that need to be done, and helps you determine your priorities about gearings, components, and money, so that you will be able to perform the necessary tasks in a time-efficient manner.

The six items that need to be done to select a new gearing are listed below, but not necessarily in the order in which they are to be performed. Items (1) and (2) are *gearing decisions* which usually require a considerable amount of "gearing time" to make.

(1)   Determine the *features* of the gearing you want (high gear, low gear, number of speeds, etc.). This will be discussed more fully later in this chapter.

(2)   Look in the appendices for a gearing close to the one you want, then modify it to your requirements by changing some of the chainrings and cogs by one or two teeth.

Items (3) - (6) are *component decisions* which require "component time" to make.

(3)   Decide which components you are *willing* to replace to obtain a new gearing.

(4)   Determine which components are *available* that will operate your new gearing.

(5)   Determine the *specifications* of the available components.

(6)   Choose the exact components that you will use.

The most efficient order for you to do the above tasks is determined by the components available to you and the priorities you place on gearings, components, and money. If you are not careful, you can waste hours of time selecting a new gearing only to find that it requires components that are unavailable, too expensive, or unappealing. Two approaches will be discussed, but you may find that some variation or combination of these is best for you.

THE GEARING-FIRST APPROACH

Ideally, the most efficient order of events in selecting a new gearing is first to make the gearing decisions, and then the component decisions. This approach places the highest priority on the gearing and assumes that you are able to obtain, and willing to replace, all necessary components to get the gearing you want; if so, this is the most efficient approach for you to take.

The advantage of the gearing-first approach is that you can go to a bicycle dealer and say, "Here is the gearing I want. What components do you have, or can you get, that will enable me to install this gearing?" Dealers usually are willing to help you with this task because they want to sell components.

The disadvantage of the gearing-first approach is that you risk wasting a large amount of "gearing time." If you have spent hours of time choosing a gearing, it can be discouraging to find that you need components which are unavailable, unappealing, or beyond your budget, and that you must begin all over.

Actually there is no such thing as a pure gearing-first approach to selecting a new gearing since it is always necessary to stay within the limits imposed by the current technology. For instance, you can't have a 40T rear cog if none is manufactured. Within these limits a gearing-first approach is possible, and sometimes efficient, but many people choose either a components-first approach, or some sequence which alternates gearing and component priorities.

THE COMPONENTS-FIRST APPROACH

The components-first approach to selecting a new gearing requires that you determine, in order, (1) the components you are willing to replace, (2) the components available through dealers or catalogs, and (3) the specifications of the components you are likely to use. Then, working within the limits of these components and their specifications, you look for a gearing which has the features you want. When you finally decide upon a particular gearing, most likely it can be obtained, with components you like, within your budget. This approach places a slightly higher priority on components and money than on gearing; if necessary, be willing to make a few compromises in your gearing in order to stay within your budget or to use components you like.

Anyone who places a high priority on components will find the components-first approach effective. This includes the many riders who insist on having one particular brand of components, tourists who consider it important to use components for which they have the knowledge and tools to repair, and those cyclists who wish to stay within the same indexed shifting system that is already on their bicycles.

If you have an indexed system, simply ask your dealer for the specifications of the few components compatible with it, and look for a gearing within those limits. If you plan to use a friction system, you have more choices (at this time, anyway) and it will take longer to determine which components you are likely to use. In this case, it helps to have first determined some *general* information about the gearing you want, especially its approximate range. For instance, if you want a wide-range gearing, you will need a triple crankset with especially small chainrings, a freewheel with large cogs, a rear derailleur with a large wrap-up capacity, and a large capacity front derailleur. With this type of information in mind, go to your dealer and ask to examine current copies of manufacturers' catalogs. Identify a few appealing models of each component you are willing to replace which meet your general requirements, verify that they are available through your dealer, and take some notes about their specifications. Then go home and look for the gearing you want within these limits.

It is not the purpose of this book to recommend brands or models. An excellent source for specifics on particular models of gearing components are the magazine articles written by Frank Berto of *Bicycling* magazine. A recognized authority on bicycle technology, his articles and book (see Further Reading) provide valuable information about the latest designs of gearing components.

DETERMINING GEARING FEATURES

Before actually looking for a specific gearing, you need to make preliminary decisions, usually in this order, about these features: (1) highest gear, (2) lowest gear, (3) number of speeds, (4) type of gearing (Half-step, Crossover, etc.), (5) base gear(s), and (6) start-up gear(s). These are the decisions which make the gearing *your* gearing, one which *you* derive satisfaction in using, because you know it has been chosen *by you* to fit *your* body, *your* terrain, *your* philosophy of shifting, and *your* reasons for riding. While you might discuss certain aspects with friends, to get full satisfaction from your new gearing you must make these decisions *yourself*. (Since this is somewhat time-consuming and involves only personal preferences and priorities, bicycle dealers usually prefer that you make these decisions without their help.)

HIGHEST GEAR

For recreational purposes, your highest gear should be between 85 and 100 inches. Think about the highest gear on your present gearing. Do you use it often, and do you frequently find yourself wanting a higher gear? Do you seldom use it and would you be satisfied if it were lower? In fact, would you use it more often if it were lower? Your answers to these questions will determine your preliminary feelings about a highest gear.

Try to avoid the common mistake of talking yourself into having a highest gear that is too high. There is a certain "macho" aura attached to gears of 100 inches or more, and their inclusion is often "justified" with an argument about wanting them available for the few times when they are needed. For most riders there are more reasons for the highest gear to be *lower* than 100-inch than for it to be higher. The first such reason is that it wastes a potentially useful gear, especially if you like to coast downhill. In this case you use your highest gear only with a tailwind on nearly level terrain. The formulas in Appendix J produce the following information:

Gear-inches	Cadence	Speed
100	80 rpm	24 mph
96	80 rpm	23 mph
93	80 rpm	22 mph

How often, and for how long, do you actually propel yourself with a cadence of 80 rpm, at 24 mph? Would you be just as satisfied going 23 or 22 mph? If so, you would be better off with a 93-inch gear that you could use more often.

Knee strain is the second reason for having a highest gear that is lower than 100 inches. If your highest gear is 100-inch or higher, you must exercise great restraint to avoid using it with a low 60-70 rpm cadence — a combination which many people find tempting, but which can damage their knees. A 93-inch gear with a 76 rpm cadence produces the same 21 mph as a 100-inch gear at 70 rpm (see below), and is easier on your knees. For those brief periods when you "must" go 24 mph, couldn't you sustain a cadence of 87 rpm?

Gear-inches	Cadence	Speed
100	70 rpm	21 mph
100	65 rpm	19 mph
93	76 rpm	21 mph
93	69 rpm	19 mph
93	87 rpm	24 mph

The last reason for choosing a highest gear lower than 100 inches is that it reduces the required wrap-up of the gearing. With 27-inch wheels, by having a 93-inch highest gear rather than 100-inch, you save either 3T or 4T of required wrap-up (depending upon whether you have a 13T or 14T smallest cog). This is important if you want a lowest gear near 20 inches and wish to avoid exceeding the wrap-up capacity of the rear derailleur.

Gears higher than 100 inches are for riders who *know* that they have need of such gears; other cyclists should seriously consider the 85- to 95-inch range for their highest gears. At this stage of the gearing selection process, you need not determine exactly your highest gear, but at least decide upon a 5- or 6-inch range you are likely to use. When you examine specific gearings you can make your final choice.

LOWEST GEAR

Your lowest gear should be chosen with more care than your highest gear. If your highest gear isn't high enough, occasionally you will suffer the minor inconvenience of having to go slower than necessary, but you *will* reach your destination without dismounting and without damaging your body. However, if your lowest gear is not low enough, it is likely that you will damage your knees every time you pedal up a tough hill. On these hills, you *know* you can make it to the top if you just reduce your cadence enough to avoid becoming out-of-breath. Your knees don't hurt now (the pain comes later), you are out to *ride,* not walk, your bike, and the hill is a challenge which everyone else seems to be conquering safely. You *should* walk uphill on these occasions, but you don't. With a lower gear you could safely ride up more such hills.

The lowest gear readily obtainable at the present time (for 27-inch wheels) is a 19-inch gear, achieved with a 24T chainring, 34T cog, and a rear derailleur with a 34T largest-cog capacity. If wrap-up is a problem, consider using a 32T cog; this will save 2T of wrap-up, and you won't feel the difference between the 20-inch gear it produces and the 19-inch gear.

Mountain bikers usually want especially low gears; they are out to challenge hills and expect to do so often. Tourists usually like to be prepared with low gears because of the added weight they carry and the uncertainty of the terrain they will encounter. At the other extreme, triathlon competitors often have a lowest gear between 40 and 60 inches. Think about the terrain on which you will ride, the lowest gear on your present gearing, how often you use it, and make your new choice accordingly; if there is doubt in your mind, go with the lower choice. You don't need to determine your exact choice now, but try to decide upon upper and lower limits for the lowest gear you want.

NUMBER OF SPEEDS

You need enough speeds to enable you to find a primary shift sequence *of the type you like* which will take you from your lowest gear to your highest using only half- and full-steps of change. So the range of your gearing determines, in part, the number of speeds to have: the wider the range, the more speeds you need. The other factor is *shifting convenience:* you want to provide yourself with enough speeds so that you can have the type of primary shift sequence you like. Usually this amounts to deciding whether you want a Half-step sequence with its many 1-cog double-shifts, or a Crossover sequence containing only single-shifts.

If you like the Half-step shift sequence (which includes all 10 or 12 gears), you need either a Half-step or a C(HS) gearing. With a 13T or 14T smallest cog, Half-step gearings, whether 10 or 12 speeds, are limited in range to about 65 gear-inches (35-100, 33-96, etc.). For this range, 10 speeds are sufficient; you can have 12 speeds, but unless you go to an 11T or 12T cog, you won't widen the range by doing so — you will just have smaller steps. However, you can widen the range (somewhat) by using a C(HS) gearing. If you want a Half-step + Granny gearing, you may be happier with 18 speeds rather than 15, so that you can avoid the use of the extreme chain deflection gear in the lower right corner of your matrix and still have a 10-speed Half-step gearing in the remaining portion of the center and right columns.

If you are a "single shifter," and prefer one of the Single-shift Crossover patterns, whether to be used with a Crossover or Half-step gearing, you will be much happier with six cogs rather than five. The 10-speed Single-shift Crossover pattern contains only 6 gears — not enough for most gearings. The 12-speed Dual-option Crossover strategy has 8 gears in its primary sequence, which is usually sufficient even for those Crossover gearings in which the range is about 30 to 100 inches. For the same reasons, 18-speeds are preferable to 15-speeds if you want Granny gears along with (primarily) single-shifts.

For genuine off-pavement mountain bike riding, you want 15 or 18 speeds (or more, when available) just to get the Granny gears you need. Most mountain bikes are made to accept the standard-width 6-cog freewheel, and for these bikes an 18-speed gearing is the logical choice. For other mountain bikes, you can choose between a 15-speed gearing with a standard-width freewheel, or an 18-speed gearing using an ultra-narrow freewheel. If you are going to use the independent-column strategy of shifting for off-pavement riding, it doesn't matter much whether you have five or six gears in each column; it would be nicer to have six, but you will be almost as happy with five.

14-speed gearings are now used regularly by racers but their 21-speed recreational counterparts are still extremely rare. 8-cog hubs have just become available, but little is known of their actual performance other than manufacturers' claims. If you opt for 16-, 21-, or even 24-speeds in the near future, be prepared to accept the consequences of mechanical problems yet unknown. Magazines can keep you up-to-date about this topic.

TYPE OF GEARING

The manner in which you expect to use your bike helps to determine the type of gearing you want. Half-step + Granny and Double Crossover gearings are the popular choices if you have need of a wide-range gearing for use on pavement; you choose between them according to how you like to shift. For off-pavement mountain bike use, Alpine + Granny gearings and some Double Crossover gearings shift well with the independent-column strategy.

If you are selecting a 10- or 12-speed gearing, your choice of lowest gear will be a factor in determining the type of gearing you need. With a 13T or 14T smallest cog, Half-step gearings limit your lowest gear to about 35 inches, Alpine and Crossover gearings take you down to about 30 inches, and you need a Wide-step gearing (with its large changes between chainrings) to go lower.

BASE GEAR

Your base gear should feel comfortable on nearly level pavement with a mild wind resistance. (If your riding is almost all on hills, you can disregard the notion of a base gear.) Under the assumption that you need such a gear, it should be between 50 and 70 inches, and the best way to choose it is through experience. What gear do you now use during base gear conditions? Does it feel comfortable? Should it be higher? Lower?

You can also use speed and cadence to select a base gear. How fast do you normally go during base gear conditions and what cadence do you *want* to have in this gear? Use Appendix J to select your base gear accordingly. For instance, if your experience shows that you normally go 14 mph in base gear conditions, and you want to make sure you have a cadence of 80 rpm, you will need a 59-inch base gear. This is also a way to force yourself to increase your cadence. If you are presently doing 14 mph in a 65-inch base gear, you are doing so with a cadence of only 72 rpm. By switching to the 59-inch base gear you force yourself to learn to pedal at 80 rpm to maintain your 14 mph speed.

START-UP GEARS

Start-up gears, whether achieved with left- or right-handed downshifts from the base gears, are usually given lowest priority among gearing features. This is probably because, in any reasonable gearing, there is always *some* gear appropriate for start-up purposes, and it doesn't matter much if it is a little too high or too low because it is used for only a few seconds.

If you plan to use your bike primarily for city riding, such as shopping or commuting, you might wish to give start-up gears a high priority. With your present gearing, determine the approximate size of the start-up gears which feel comfortable to you, choose the matrix positions in which you wish to have them, and look for an appropriate gearing.

REVIEW OF TECHNICAL CONSIDERATIONS

Use the 18-speed chart shown below to review the technical considerations that must be kept in mind as you seek your gearing, especially if you are using a components-first approach. Capital letters represent chainring and cog tooth numbers; lower-case letters represent the gears and/or their positions.

	G	H	I
A	a	b	c
B	d	e	f
C	g	h	i
D	j	k	l
E	m	n	o
F	p	q	r

Because of chain deflection, **a** and **r**, and possibly **d** and **o**, will probably be disregarded.

Positions **h** and **k**, with minimum chain deflection, are the best places to have a base gear or dual base gears.

The lowest gear, **p**, is determined by the smallest chainring G and the largest cog F. If it is an absolute requirement that **p** be as small as possible, G needs to be the smallest of the available chainrings and F the largest of the available cogs.

The highest gear, **c**, is determined by the largest chainring I and the smallest cog A.

The difference between I and G must be no more than the capacity of the front derailleur. So if the lowest gear has already been determined, and G is therefore known, I is limited by the capacity of the front derailleur. For instance, if a 24T chainring has been chosen for G, and the front derailleur has a capacity of 26T, then chainring I can be no more than 50T.

The required wrap-up of this gearing is (I-G) + (F-A). If this is more than the wrap-up capacity of the rear derailleur, then either the long-chain method or the short-chain method of exceeding the rear derailleur wrap-up capacity must be used. If the long-chain method is used, gear **a**, and possibly gears **d** and **g**, will need to be avoided as they will produce more excess chain than the rear derailleur can wrap up. *Use of these gears could be dangerous.* If the short-chain method is used, there will not be enough chain to shift into gear **r**, and possibly gears **o** and **q**. *Attempts to shift into these gears could be dangerous.* These problems can be avoided by decreasing the required wrap-up.

Approximately 3T of required wrap-up can be saved by using a smallest cog of 13T rather than 14T. Gearings R and S both range from 19 to 100 inches, but the required wrap-up of Gearing S is only 45T instead of the 48T for Gearing R, as shown below.

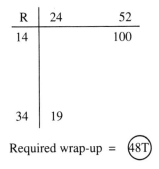

R	24	52
14		100
34	19	

Required wrap-up = (48T)

101

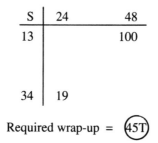

Another 2T of required wrap-up can be saved by having a 20-inch lowest gear rather than one of 19 inches, as shown in Gearing T, below.

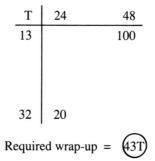

Better yet, reduce your highest gear and learn to pedal faster; you will save your knees as well as a few more teeth of required wrap-up. See Gearing U, below.

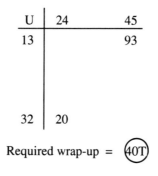

For 15- and 18-speed gearings, the difference between I and H must be considered when choosing a front derailleur. (See the discussion of large capacity front derailleurs in Chapter 6.)

LOOKING FOR YOUR GEARING

The extensive appendices are included to provide a base from which you may start your search for a gearing. With the gearing-first approach, you begin your search immediately after determining the features you want. With the components-first approach, you use the appendices last, after also determining the specifications of the components you are likely to use.

Try to determine your priorities about gearing features before you actually use the appendices. You can save time by deciding in advance those features on which you will compromise and those on which you will not.

Begin your search by looking for gearings which contain most of the features you want. (With the components-first approach, you consider only those gearings which are possible to obtain with the components that are likely to be used.) Circle, or identify in some other way, those gearings which appeal to you so that you easily can find them later. You might even make notes about the advantages and disadvantages of each such gearing, so that you won't have to totally "re-think" the gearing each time you look at it.

Next, try modifying those gearings you have selected by altering a few cogs and chainrings by one or two teeth to see if you can get exactly what you want. Use the gear-inch chart on page 27 to modify the gearings for 27-inch/700mm wheels (Appendices A-D) and use the chart on page 28 to modify the gearings for 26-inch wheels (Appendices E-H).

If you are lucky, you will find your perfect gearing quickly. More likely though, you will need to spend a few hours examining and modifying gearings. This is the part that only you can do, because only you know why a particular gearing isn't perfect, and only you can say that one gearing is better than another. But *you* are the one who gets the reward of owning and operating a bicycle geared just for you.

Good luck, and happy pedaling!

APPENDICES

ABOUT THE APPENDICES

Gearings in the same appendix are listed numerically, first by the number of teeth on the cogs, and then by the number of teeth on the chainrings. Each gearing is identified by type using the following abbreviations:

A	Alpine	A+G	Alpine plus Granny
C	Crossover	DC	Double Crossover
HS	Half-step	HS+G	Half-step plus Granny
WS	Wide-step		

C(HS)   A **Crossover** gearing having the **Half-step** zig-zag shift sequence. The percentages prevent this from being a true Half-step gearing.

DC(HS)   A **Double Crossover** gearing in which the middle and outer chainrings produce a **C(HS)** gearing.

C(A)   A **Crossover** gearing having the **Alpine** shift sequence. The percentages prevent this from being a true Alpine gearing.

DC(A)   A **Double Crossover** gearing in which the middle and outer chainrings produce a **C(A)** gearing.

Immediately following the type of gearing is the **required wrap-up** of the gearing, measured in number of teeth (T).

ITEMS TO KEEP IN MIND

* For bicycles having 700-mm rims and tires, gearings for 27-inch wheels should be used.

* Any gearing, regardless of type, may be shifted in any desired manner.

* Alpine gearings are frequently used with a Crossover shift sequence because the Alpine sequence is difficult to learn and to perform.

* Many riders prefer the Half-step shift sequence even though it contains many 1-cog double-shifts.

* Riders who prefer to use a Single-shift Crossover strategy should consider Half-step gearings as well as Crossover and Alpine gearings. Many Half-step gearings work well when used with a Crossover shift sequence. Many 12-speed Half-step gearings shift nicely with the Dual-option Crossover strategy.

A: 10-SPEED GEARINGS 27-INCH WHEELS

	39	48
13	81	100
15	70	86
18	59	72
22	48	59
26	41	50

C, 22T

	40	48
13	83	100
15	72	86
18	60	72
22	49	59
26	42	50

C, 21T

	40	50
13	83	104
15	72	90
18	60	75
22	49	61
26	42	52

A, 23T

	40	50
13	83	104
15	72	90
18	60	75
22	49	61
27	40	50

C(A), 24T

	40	48
13	83	100
15	72	86
18	60	72
22	49	59
30	36	43

C, 25T

	44	48
13	91	100
15	79	86
18	66	72
22	54	59
30	40	43

C(HS), 21T

	46	50
13	96	104
15	83	90
18	69	75
22	56	61
30	41	45

C(HS), 21T

	32	48
13	66	100
15	58	86
18	48	72
23	38	56
31	28	42

WS, 34T

	30	48
13	62	100
15	54	86
18	45	72
24	34	54
32	25	41

WS, 37T

	30	48
13	62	100
15	54	86
18	45	72
24	34	54
34	24	38

WS, 39T

	30	48
13	62	100
15	54	86
18	45	72
25	32	52
34	24	38

WS, 39T

	39	50
13	81	104
16	66	84
19	55	71
23	46	59
28	38	48

A, 26T

	40	48
13	83	100
16	68	81
19	57	68
23	47	56
28	39	46

C, 23T

	44	48
13	91	100
16	74	81
19	63	68
23	52	56
28	42	46

HS, 19T

	46	50
13	96	104
16	78	84
19	65	71
23	54	59
28	44	48

HS, 19T

	40	50
13	83	104
16	68	84
19	57	71
24	45	56
31	35	44

C, 28T

	43	48
13	89	100
16	73	81
19	61	68
24	48	54
32	36	41

C(HS), 24T

	44	48
13	91	100
16	74	81
19	63	68
24	50	54
32	37	41

C(HS), 23T

	45	50
13	93	104
16	76	84
19	64	71
24	51	56
32	38	42

C(HS), 24T

	34	48
13	71	100
16	57	81
20	46	65
24	38	54
30	31	43

WS, 31T

	36	48
13	75	100
16	61	81
20	49	65
24	41	54
30	32	43

A, 29T

	38	50
13	79	104
16	64	84
20	51	68
24	43	56
30	34	45

A, 29T

	40	48
13	83	100
16	68	81
20	54	65
24	45	54
30	36	43

C, 25T

	43	48
13	89	100
16	73	81
20	58	65
24	48	54
30	39	43

HS, 22T

	45	50
13	93	104
16	76	84
20	61	68
24	51	56
30	41	45

HS, 22T

	37	50
13	77	104
16	62	84
20	50	68
25	40	54
32	31	42

A, 32T

	40	48
13	83	100
16	68	81
20	54	65
25	43	52
32	34	41

C(HS), 27T

	43	48
13	89	100
16	73	81
20	58	65
25	46	52
32	36	41

HS, 24T

	45	50
13	93	104
16	76	84
20	61	68
25	49	54
32	38	42

HS, 24T

	36	50
13	75	104
16	61	84
20	49	68
26	37	52
34	29	40

A, 35T

	38	48
13	79	100
16	64	81
20	51	65
26	39	50
34	30	38

C, 31T

	38	50
13	79	104
16	64	84
20	51	68
26	39	52
34	30	40

C(A), 33T

	43	48
13	89	100
16	73	81
20	58	65
26	45	50
34	34	38

HS, 26T

	45	50
13	93	104
16	76	84
20	61	68
26	47	52
34	36	40

HS, 26T

	36	52
14	69	100
15	65	94
17	57	83
20	49	70
26	37	54

WS, 28T

	42	52
14	81	100
16	71	88
18	63	78
21	54	67
28	41	50

C, 24T

	46	50
14	89	96
16	78	84
19	65	71
22	56	61
30	41	45

C(HS), 20T

	48	52
14	93	100
16	81	88
19	68	74
22	59	64
30	43	47

C(HS), 20T

	34	52
14	66	100
16	57	88
19	48	74
23	40	61
28	33	50

WS, 32T

	42	52
14	81	100
16	71	88
19	60	74
23	49	61
28	41	50

C(A), 24T

	42	52
14	81	100
16	71	88
19	60	74
23	49	61
30	38	47

C, 26T

	40	50
14	77	96
16	68	84
19	57	71
24	45	56
28	39	48

C, 24T

	42	52
14	81	100
16	71	88
19	60	74
24	47	59
28	41	50

C, 24T

	30	52
14	58	100
16	51	88
19	43	74
24	34	59
32	25	44

WS, 40T

	32	52
14	62	100
16	54	88
19	45	74
24	36	59
32	27	44

WS, 38T

	40	50
14	77	96
16	68	84
19	57	71
24	45	56
32	34	42

C, 28T

	42	52
14	81	100
16	71	88
19	60	74
24	47	59
32	35	44

C, 28T

	40	50
14	77	96
16	68	84
19	57	71
24	45	56
34	32	40

C, 30T

	40	52
14	77	100
16	68	88
19	57	74
24	45	59
34	32	41

C, 32T

	42	52
14	81	100
16	71	88
19	60	74
24	47	59
34	33	41

C, 30T

	30	52
14	58	100
16	51	88
19	43	74
25	32	56
34	24	41

WS, 42T

	40	50
14	77	96
16	68	84
19	57	71
25	43	54
34	32	40

C, 30T

	40	52
14	77	100
16	68	88
19	57	74
25	43	56
34	32	41

C, 32T

	42	50
14	81	96
16	71	84
19	60	71
25	45	54
34	33	40

C, 28T

	42	52
14	81	100
16	71	88
19	60	74
25	45	56
34	33	41

C, 30T

	39	50
14	75	96
17	62	79
20	53	68
24	44	56
28	38	48

A, 25T

	39	52
14	75	100
17	62	83
20	53	70
24	44	59
28	38	50

A, 27T

	40	50
14	77	96
17	64	79
20	54	68
24	45	56
28	39	48

C(A), 24T

	40	52
14	77	100
17	64	83
20	54	70
24	45	59
28	39	50

A, 26T

	42	52
14	81	100
17	67	83
20	57	70
24	47	59
28	41	50

C(A), 24T

	45	50
14	87	96
17	71	79
20	61	68
24	51	56
28	43	48

HS, 19T

	46	50
14	89	96
17	73	79
20	62	68
24	52	56
28	44	48

HS, 18T

	47	52
14	91	100
17	75	83
20	63	70
24	53	59
28	45	50

HS, 19T

	48	52
14	93	100
17	76	83
20	65	70
24	54	59
28	46	50

HS, 18T

	39	52
14	75	100
17	62	83
20	53	70
24	44	59
30	35	47

A, 29T

	45	50
14	87	96
17	71	79
20	61	68
24	51	56
30	41	45

HS, 21T

	47	52
14	91	100
17	75	83
20	63	70
24	53	59
30	42	47

HS, 21T

	38	52
14	73	100
17	60	83
21	49	67
26	39	54
32	32	44

A, 32T

	43	48
14	83	93
17	68	76
21	55	62
26	45	50
32	36	41

HS, 23T

	45	50
14	87	96
17	71	79
21	58	64
26	47	52
32	38	42

HS, 23T

	47	52
14	91	100
17	75	83
21	60	67
26	49	54
32	40	44

HS, 23T

	44	50
14	85	96
17	70	79
21	57	64
26	46	52
34	35	40

HS, 26T

	45	50
14	87	96
17	71	79
21	58	64
26	47	52
34	36	40

HS, 25T

	46	50
14	89	96
17	73	79
21	59	64
26	48	52
34	37	40

C(HS), 24T

	47	52
14	91	100
17	75	83
21	60	67
26	49	54
34	37	41

HS, 25T

B: 12-SPEED GEARINGS
27-INCH WHEELS

	40	50
13	83	104
14	77	96
16	68	84
19	57	71
23	47	59
28	39	48

C, 25T

	32	48
13	66	100
14	62	93
16	54	81
19	45	68
24	36	54
31	28	42

WS, 34T

	32	48
13	66	100
14	62	93
16	54	81
19	45	68
25	35	52
34	25	38

WS, 37T

	34	48
13	71	100
14	66	93
16	57	81
19	48	68
25	37	52
34	27	38

WS, 35T

	38	46
13	79	96
15	68	83
17	60	73
19	54	65
25	41	50
32	32	39

C, 27T

	39	48
13	81	100
15	70	86
17	62	76
19	55	68
25	42	52
32	33	41

C, 28T

	40	48
13	83	100
15	72	86
17	64	76
19	57	68
25	43	52
32	34	41

C, 27T

	42	50
13	87	104
15	76	90
17	67	79
19	60	71
25	45	54
32	35	42

C, 27T

	37	46
13	77	96
15	67	83
17	59	73
19	53	65
25	40	50
34	29	37

C, 30T

	38	46
13	79	96
15	68	83
17	60	73
19	54	65
25	41	50
34	30	37

C, 29T

	39	48
13	81	100
15	70	86
17	62	76
19	55	68
25	42	52
34	31	38

C, 30T

	40	48
13	83	100
15	72	86
17	64	76
19	57	68
25	43	52
34	32	38

C, 29T

	42	50
13	87	104
15	76	90
17	67	79
19	60	71
25	45	54
34	33	40

C, 29T

	44	48
13	91	100
15	79	86
17	70	76
19	63	68
25	48	52
34	35	38

C(HS), 25T

	37	46
13	77	96
15	67	83
17	59	73
19	53	65
26	38	48
34	29	37

C, 30T

	39	48
13	81	100
15	70	86
17	62	76
19	55	68
26	41	50
34	31	38

C, 30T

	40	48
13	83	100
15	72	86
17	64	76
19	57	68
26	42	50
34	32	38

C, 29T

	44	48
13	91	100
15	79	86
17	70	76
19	63	68
26	46	50
34	35	38

C(HS), 25T

	40	50
13	83	104
15	72	90
17	64	79
20	54	68
23	47	59
26	42	52

A, 23T

	39	48
13	81	100
15	70	86
17	62	76
20	53	65
24	44	54
28	38	46

C(A), 24T

	39	50
13	81	104
15	70	90
17	62	79
20	53	68
24	44	56
28	38	48

A, 26T

	40	48
13	83	100
15	72	86
17	64	76
20	54	65
24	45	54
28	39	46

C, 23T

	42	46
13	87	96
15	76	83
17	67	73
20	57	62
24	47	52
28	41	44

HS, 19T

	44	48
13	91	100
15	79	86
17	70	76
20	59	65
24	50	54
28	42	46

HS, 19T

	46	50
13	96	104
15	83	90
17	73	79
20	62	68
24	52	56
28	44	48

HS, 19T

	30	48
13	62	100
15	54	86
17	48	76
20	41	65
25	32	52
34	24	38

WS, 39T

	38	46
13	79	96
15	68	83
17	60	73
20	51	62
25	41	50
34	30	37

C, 29T

	38	48
13	79	100
15	68	86
17	60	76
20	51	65
25	41	52
34	30	38

C, 31T

	39	48
13	81	100
15	70	86
17	62	76
20	53	65
25	42	52
34	31	38

C, 30T

	40	48
13	83	100
15	72	86
17	64	76
20	54	65
25	43	52
34	32	38

C, 29T

	40	48
13	83	100
15	72	86
17	64	76
22	49	59
26	42	50
34	32	38

C, 29T

	38	50
13	79	104
15	68	90
18	57	75
21	49	64
25	41	54
30	34	45

A, 29T

	39	48
13	81	100
15	70	86
18	59	72
21	50	62
25	42	52
30	35	43

C(A), 26T

	42	46
13	87	96
15	76	83
18	63	69
21	54	59
25	45	50
30	38	41

HS, 21T

	44	48
13	91	100
15	79	86
18	66	72
21	57	62
25	48	52
30	40	43

HS, 21T

	46	50
13	96	104
15	83	90
18	69	75
21	59	64
25	50	54
30	41	45

HS, 21T

	40	52
13	83	108
16	68	88
19	57	74
22	49	64
26	42	54
32	34	44

A, 31T

	42	46
13	87	96
16	71	78
19	60	65
22	52	56
26	44	48
32	35	39

HS, 23T

	42	52
13	87	108
16	71	88
19	60	74
22	52	64
26	44	54
32	35	44

C, 29T

	44	48
13	91	100
16	74	81
19	63	68
22	54	59
26	46	50
32	37	41

HS, 23T

	46	50
13	96	104
16	78	84
19	65	71
22	56	61
26	48	52
32	39	42

HS, 23T

	36	48
13	75	100
16	61	81
19	51	68
22	44	59
27	36	48
32	30	41

A, 31T

	38	50
13	79	104
16	64	84
19	54	71
22	47	61
27	38	50
32	32	42

A, 31T

	42	46
13	87	96
16	71	78
19	60	65
22	52	56
27	42	46
32	35	39

HS, 23T

	43	48
13	89	100
16	73	81
19	61	68
22	53	59
27	43	48
32	36	41

HS, 24T

	44	48
13	91	100
16	74	81
19	63	68
22	54	59
27	44	48
32	37	41

HS, 23T

	45	50
13	93	104
16	76	84
19	64	71
22	55	61
27	45	50
32	38	42

HS, 24T

	41	46
13	85	96
16	69	78
19	58	65
22	50	56
27	41	46
34	33	37

HS, 26T

	42	46
13	87	96
16	71	78
19	60	65
22	52	56
27	42	46
34	33	37

HS, 25T

	44	48
13	91	100
16	74	81
19	63	68
22	54	59
27	44	48
34	35	38

HS, 25T

	37	50
13	77	104
16	62	84
19	53	71
23	43	59
28	36	48
34	29	40

A, 34T

	43	48
13	89	100
16	73	81
19	61	68
23	50	56
28	41	46
34	34	38

HS, 26T

	45	50
13	93	104
16	76	84
19	64	71
23	53	59
28	43	48
34	36	40

HS, 26T

	34	52
14	66	100
15	61	94
17	54	83
20	46	70
23	40	61
28	33	50

WS, 32T

	42	52
14	81	100
15	76	94
17	67	83
20	57	70
23	49	61
28	41	50

C, 24T

	44	52
14	85	100
15	79	94
17	70	83
20	59	70
23	52	61
28	42	50

C, 22T

	40	52
14	77	100
15	72	94
17	64	83
20	54	70
24	45	59
28	39	50

C, 26T

	32	52
14	62	100
15	58	94
17	51	83
20	43	70
25	35	56
32	27	44

WS, 38T

	42	52
14	81	100
15	76	94
17	67	83
20	57	70
25	45	56
32	35	44

C, 28T

	34	52
14	66	100
15	61	94
17	54	83
20	46	70
26	35	54
34	27	41

WS, 38T

	40	50
14	77	96
16	68	84
18	60	75
21	51	64
24	45	56
28	39	48

A, 24T

	42	52
14	81	100
16	71	88
18	63	78
21	54	67
24	47	59
28	41	50

A, 24T

	36	52
14	69	100
16	61	88
18	54	78
21	46	67
25	39	56
31	31	45

WS, 33T

	34	52
14	66	100
16	57	88
18	51	78
21	44	67
26	35	54
32	29	44

WS, 36T

	32	52
14	62	100
16	54	88
18	48	78
21	41	67
26	33	54
34	25	41

WS, 40T

	40	48
14	77	93
16	68	81
18	60	72
21	51	62
26	42	50
34	32	38

C, 28T

	40	50
14	77	96
16	68	84
18	60	75
21	51	64
26	42	52
34	32	40

C, 30T

	42	50
14	81	96
16	71	84
18	63	75
21	54	64
26	44	52
34	33	40

C, 28T

	42	52
14	81	100
16	71	88
18	63	78
21	54	67
26	44	54
34	33	41

C, 30T

	40	50
14	77	96
16	68	84
19	57	71
22	49	61
26	42	52
30	36	45

A, 26T

	40	52
14	77	100
16	68	88
19	57	74
22	49	64
26	42	54
30	36	47

A, 28T

	41	52
14	79	100
16	69	88
19	58	74
22	50	64
26	43	54
30	37	47

A, 27T

	42	52
14	81	100
16	71	88
19	60	74
22	52	64
26	44	54
30	38	47

A, 26T

	43	52
14	83	100
16	73	88
19	61	74
22	53	64
26	45	54
30	39	47

C(A), 25T

	46	50
14	89	96
16	78	84
19	65	71
22	56	61
26	48	52
30	41	45

HS, 20T

	48	52
14	93	100
16	81	88
19	68	74
22	59	64
26	50	54
30	43	47

HS, 20T

	38	48
14	73	93
16	64	81
19	54	68
22	47	59
26	39	50
32	32	41

C(A), 28T

	40	50
14	77	96
16	68	84
19	57	71
22	49	61
26	42	52
32	34	42

C, 28T

	40	52
14	77	100
16	68	88
19	57	74
22	49	64
26	42	54
32	34	44

A, 30T

	41	52
14	79	100
16	69	88
19	58	74
22	50	64
26	43	54
32	35	44

C(A), 29T

	42	52
14	81	100
16	71	88
19	60	74
22	52	64
26	44	54
32	35	44

C, 28T

	46	50
14	89	96
16	78	84
19	65	71
22	56	61
26	48	52
32	39	42

HS, 22T

	48	52
14	93	100
16	81	88
19	68	74
22	59	64
26	50	54
32	41	44

HS, 22T

	30	52
14	58	100
16	51	88
19	43	74
22	37	64
26	31	54
34	24	41

WS, 42T

	32	52
14	62	100
16	54	88
19	45	74
22	39	64
26	33	54
34	25	41

WS, 40T

	40	52
14	77	100
16	68	88
19	57	74
22	49	64
26	42	54
34	32	41

C, 32T

	42	52
14	81	100
16	71	88
19	60	74
22	52	64
26	44	54
34	33	41

C, 30T

	43	52
14	83	100
16	73	88
19	61	74
22	53	64
26	45	54
34	34	41

C, 29T

	46	50
14	89	96
16	78	84
19	65	71
22	56	61
26	48	52
34	37	40

C(HS), 24T

	48	52
14	93	100
16	81	88
19	68	74
22	59	64
26	50	54
34	38	41

C(HS), 24T

	41	52
14	79	100
16	69	88
19	58	74
23	48	61
27	41	52
32	35	44

A, 29T

	46	50
14	89	96
16	78	84
19	65	71
23	54	59
27	46	50
32	39	42

HS, 22T

	48	52
14	93	100
16	81	88
19	68	74
23	56	61
27	48	52
32	41	44

HS, 22T

	40	52
14	77	100
17	64	83
20	54	70
24	45	59
27	40	52
34	32	41

A, 32T

	46	50
14	89	96
17	73	79
20	62	68
24	52	56
27	46	50
34	37	40

HS, 24T

	48	52
14	93	100
17	76	83
20	65	70
24	54	59
27	48	52
34	38	41

HS, 24T

	40	52
14	77	100
17	64	83
20	54	70
24	45	59
28	39	50
34	32	41

A, 32T

	45	50
14	87	96
17	71	79
20	61	68
24	51	56
28	43	48
34	36	40

HS, 25T

	46	50
14	89	96
17	73	79
20	62	68
24	52	56
28	44	48
34	37	40

HS, 24T

	48	52
14	93	100
17	76	83
20	65	70
24	54	59
28	46	50
34	38	41

HS, 24T

C: 15-SPEED GEARINGS 27-INCH WHEELS

	24	40	48
13	50	83	100
15	43	72	86
18	36	60	72
22	29	49	59
26	25	42	50

DC, 37T

	24	40	48
13	50	83	100
15	43	72	86
18	36	60	72
22	29	49	59
30	22	36	43

DC, 41T

	24	44	48
13	50	91	100
15	43	79	86
18	36	66	72
22	29	54	59
30	22	40	43

DC(HS), 41T

	24	46	50
13	50	96	104
15	43	83	90
18	36	69	75
22	29	56	61
30	22	41	45

DC(HS), 43T

	28	44	48
13	58	91	100
15	50	79	86
18	42	66	72
22	34	54	59
30	25	40	43

DC(HS), 37T

	24	44	48
13	50	91	100
16	41	74	81
19	34	63	68
23	28	52	56
28	23	42	46

HS+G, 39T

	26	44	48
13	54	91	100
16	44	74	81
19	37	63	68
23	31	52	56
28	25	42	46

HS+G, 37T

	28	44	48
13	58	91	100
16	47	74	81
19	40	63	68
23	33	52	56
28	27	42	46

HS+G, 35T

	28	46	50
13	58	96	104
16	47	78	84
19	40	65	71
23	33	54	59
28	27	44	48

HS+G, 37T

	24	40	50
13	50	83	104
16	41	68	84
19	34	57	71
24	27	45	56
31	21	35	44

DC, 44T

	24	43	48
13	50	89	100
16	41	73	81
19	34	61	68
24	27	48	54
32	20	36	41

DC(HS), 43T

	24	44	48
13	50	91	100
16	41	74	81
19	34	63	68
24	27	50	54
32	20	37	41

DC(HS), 43T

	26	45	50
13	54	93	104
16	44	76	84
19	37	64	71
24	29	51	56
32	22	38	42

DC(HS), 43T

	24	36	48
13	50	75	100
16	41	61	81
20	32	49	65
24	27	41	54
30	22	32	43

A+G, 41T

	24	43	48
13	50	89	100
16	41	73	81
20	32	58	65
24	27	48	54
30	22	39	43

HS+G, 41T

	26	43	48
13	54	89	100
16	44	73	81
20	35	58	65
24	29	48	54
30	23	39	43

HS+G, 39T

	28	43	48
13	58	89	100
16	47	73	81
20	38	58	65
24	32	48	54
30	25	39	43

HS+G, 37T

	28	45	50
13	58	93	104
16	47	76	84
20	38	61	68
24	32	51	56
30	25	41	45

HS+G, 39T

	24	40	48
13	50	83	100
16	41	68	81
20	32	54	65
25	26	43	52
32	20	34	41

DC(HS), 43T

	24	43	48
13	50	89	100
16	41	73	81
20	32	58	65
25	26	46	52
32	20	36	41

HS+G, 43T

	28	43	48
13	58	89	100
16	47	73	81
20	38	58	65
25	30	46	52
32	24	36	41

HS+G, 39T

	28	45	50
13	58	93	104
16	47	76	84
20	38	61	68
25	30	49	54
32	24	38	42

HS+G, 41T

	24	38	48
13	50	79	100
16	41	64	81
20	32	51	65
26	25	39	50
34	19	30	38

DC, 45T

	24	43	48
13	50	89	100
16	41	73	81
20	32	58	65
26	25	45	50
34	19	34	38

HS+G, 45T

	26	43	48
13	54	89	100
16	44	73	81
20	35	58	65
26	27	45	50
34	21	34	38

HS+G, 43T

	28	45	50
13	58	93	104
16	47	76	84
20	38	61	68
26	29	47	52
34	22	36	40

HS+G, 43T

	24	42	52
14	46	81	100
16	41	71	88
18	36	63	78
21	31	54	67
28	23	41	50

DC, 42T

	24	46	50
14	46	89	96
16	41	78	84
19	34	65	71
22	29	56	61
30	22	41	45

DC(HS), 42T

	28	46	50
14	54	89	96
16	47	78	84
19	40	65	71
22	34	56	61
30	25	41	45

DC(HS), 38T

	28	48	52
14	54	93	100
16	47	81	88
19	40	68	74
22	34	59	64
30	25	43	47

DC(HS), 40T

	24	42	52
14	46	81	100
16	41	71	88
19	34	60	74
23	28	49	61
28	23	41	50

DC(A), 42T

	28	42	48
14	54	81	93
16	47	71	81
19	40	60	68
23	33	49	56
28	27	41	46

DC, 34T

	28	42	52
14	54	81	100
16	47	71	88
19	40	60	74
23	33	49	61
28	27	41	50

DC(A), 38T

	28	46	50
14	54	89	96
16	47	78	84
19	40	65	71
23	33	54	59
28	27	44	48

HS+G, 36T

	30	46	50
14	58	89	96
16	51	78	84
19	43	65	71
23	35	54	59
28	29	44	48

HS+"G", 34T

	24	42	52
14	46	81	100
16	41	71	88
19	34	60	74
23	28	49	61
30	22	38	47

DC, 44T

	26	42	52
14	50	81	100
16	44	71	88
19	37	60	74
23	31	49	61
30	23	38	47

DC, 42T

	28	42	52
14	54	81	100
16	47	71	88
19	40	60	74
23	33	49	61
32	24	35	44

DC, 42T

	24	40	50
14	46	77	96
16	41	68	84
19	34	57	71
24	27	45	56
28	23	39	48

DC, 40T

	24	42	52
14	46	81	100
16	41	71	88
19	34	60	74
24	27	47	59
28	23	41	50

DC, 42T

	28	40	50
14	54	77	96
16	47	68	84
19	40	57	71
24	32	45	56
28	27	39	48

DC, 36T

	28	42	48
14	54	81	93
16	47	71	81
19	40	60	68
24	32	47	54
28	27	41	46

DC, 34T

	28	42	52
14	54	81	100
16	47	71	88
19	40	60	74
24	32	47	59
28	27	41	50

DC, 38T

	26	40	50
14	50	77	96
16	44	68	84
19	37	57	71
24	29	45	56
31	23	35	44

DC, 41T

	24	40	50
14	46	77	96
16	41	68	84
19	34	57	71
24	27	45	56
32	20	34	42

DC, 44T

	28	42	52
14	54	81	100
16	47	71	88
19	40	60	74
24	32	47	59
32	24	35	44

DC, 42T

	28	42	52
14	54	81	100
16	47	71	88
19	40	60	74
24	32	47	59
34	22	33	41

DC, 44T

	24	39	50
14	46	75	96
17	38	62	79
20	32	53	68
24	27	44	56
28	23	38	48

A+G, 40T

	24	40	50
14	46	77	96
17	38	64	79
20	32	54	68
24	27	45	56
28	23	39	48

DC(A), 40T

	24	40	52
14	46	77	100
17	38	64	83
20	32	54	70
24	27	45	59
28	23	39	50

A+G, 42T

	24	45	50
14	46	87	96
17	38	71	79
20	32	61	68
24	27	51	56
28	23	43	48

HS+G, 40T

	24	46	50
14	46	89	96
17	38	73	79
20	32	62	68
24	27	52	56
28	23	44	48

HS+G, 40T

	26	40	52
14	50	77	100
17	41	64	83
20	35	54	70
24	29	45	59
28	25	39	50

A+G, 40T

	28	39	50
14	54	75	96
17	44	62	79
20	38	53	68
24	32	44	56
28	27	38	48

A+G, 36T

	28	39	52
14	54	75	100
17	44	62	83
20	38	53	70
24	32	44	59
28	27	38	50

A+G, 38T

	28	40	50
14	54	77	96
17	44	64	79
20	38	54	68
24	32	45	56
28	27	39	48

DC(A), 36T

	28	40	52
14	54	77	100
17	44	64	83
20	38	54	70
24	32	45	59
28	27	39	50

A+G, 38T

	28	42	52
14	54	81	100
17	44	67	83
20	38	57	70
24	32	47	59
28	27	41	50

DC(A), 38T

	28	45	50
14	54	87	96
17	44	71	79
20	38	61	68
24	32	51	56
28	27	43	48

HS+G, 36T

	28	45	52
14	54	87	100
17	44	71	83
20	38	61	70
24	32	51	59
28	27	43	50

DC(HS), 38T

C: 15-SPEED GEARINGS, 27-INCH WHEELS

	28	46	50
14	54	89	96
17	44	73	79
20	38	62	68
24	32	52	56
28	27	44	48

HS+G, 36T

	28	47	52
14	54	91	100
17	44	75	83
20	38	63	70
24	32	53	59
28	27	45	50

HS+G, 38T

	28	48	52
14	54	93	100
17	44	76	83
20	38	65	70
24	32	54	59
28	27	46	50

HS+G, 38T

	24	39	52
14	46	75	100
17	38	62	83
20	32	53	70
24	27	44	59
30	22	35	47

A+G, 44T

	24	45	50
14	46	87	96
17	38	71	79
20	32	61	68
24	27	51	56
30	22	41	45

HS+G, 42T

	28	45	50
14	54	87	96
17	44	71	79
20	38	61	68
24	32	51	56
30	25	41	45

HS+G, 38T

	28	47	52
14	54	91	100
17	44	75	83
20	38	63	70
24	32	53	59
30	25	42	47

HS+G, 40T

	24	43	48
14	46	83	93
17	38	68	76
21	31	55	62
26	25	45	50
32	20	36	41

HS+G, 42T

	24	45	50
14	46	87	96
17	38	71	79
21	31	58	64
26	25	47	52
32	20	38	42

HS+G, 44T

	26	45	50
14	50	87	96
17	41	71	79
21	33	58	64
26	27	47	52
32	22	38	42

HS+G, 42T

	28	43	48
14	54	83	93
17	44	68	76
21	36	55	62
26	29	45	50
32	24	36	41

HS+G, 38T

	28	45	50
14	54	87	96
17	44	71	79
21	36	58	64
26	29	47	52
32	24	38	42

HS+G, 40T

	28	47	52
14	54	91	100
17	44	75	83
21	36	60	67
26	29	49	54
32	24	40	44

HS+G, 42T

	24	45	50
14	46	87	96
17	38	71	79
21	31	58	64
26	25	47	52
34	19	36	40

HS+G, 46T

	26	43	48
14	50	83	93
17	41	68	76
21	33	55	62
26	27	45	50
34	21	34	38

HS+G, 42T

	26	45	50
14	50	87	96
17	41	71	79
21	33	58	64
26	27	47	52
34	21	36	40

HS+G, 44T

	28	44	50
14	54	85	96
17	44	70	79
21	36	57	64
26	29	46	52
34	22	35	40

HS+G, 42T

	28	45	50
14	54	87	96
17	44	71	79
21	36	58	64
26	29	47	52
34	22	36	40

HS+G, 42T

	28	46	50
14	54	89	96
17	44	73	79
21	36	59	64
26	29	48	52
34	22	37	40

DC(HS), 42T

	28	47	52
14	54	91	100
17	44	75	83
21	36	60	67
26	29	49	54
34	22	37	41

HS+G, 44T

D: 18-SPEED GEARINGS 27-INCH WHEELS

	28	45	50
13	58	93	104
14	54	87	96
17	44	71	79
20	38	61	68
24	32	51	56
28	27	43	48

DC, 37T

	24	38	46
13	50	79	96
15	43	68	83
17	38	60	73
19	34	54	65
25	26	41	50
32	20	32	39

DC, 41T

	24	39	48
13	50	81	100
15	43	70	86
17	38	62	76
19	34	55	68
25	26	42	52
32	20	33	41

DC, 43T

	24	40	48
13	50	83	100
15	43	72	86
17	38	64	76
19	34	57	68
25	26	43	52
32	20	34	41

DC, 43T

	24	42	50
13	50	87	104
15	43	76	90
17	38	67	79
19	34	60	71
25	26	45	54
32	20	35	42

DC, 45T

	26	42	50
13	54	87	104
15	47	76	90
17	41	67	79
19	37	60	71
25	28	45	54
32	22	35	42

DC, 43T

	28	40	48
13	58	83	100
15	50	72	86
17	44	64	76
19	40	57	68
25	30	43	52
32	24	34	41

DC, 39T

	24	37	46
13	50	77	96
15	43	67	83
17	38	59	73
19	34	53	65
25	26	40	50
34	19	29	37

DC, 43T

	24	38	46
13	50	79	96
15	43	68	83
17	38	60	73
19	34	54	65
25	26	41	50
34	19	30	37

DC, 43T

	24	39	48
13	50	81	100
15	43	70	86
17	38	62	76
19	34	55	68
25	26	42	52
34	19	31	38

DC, 45T

	24	40	48
13	50	83	100
15	43	72	86
17	38	64	76
19	34	57	68
25	26	43	52
34	19	32	38

DC, 45T

	24	44	48
13	50	91	100
15	43	79	86
17	38	70	76
19	34	63	68
25	26	48	52
34	19	35	38

DC(HS), 45T

	26	40	48
13	54	83	100
15	47	72	86
17	41	64	76
19	37	57	68
25	28	43	52
34	21	32	38

DC, 43T

	26	42	50
13	54	87	104
15	47	76	90
17	41	67	79
19	37	60	71
25	28	45	54
34	21	33	40

DC, 45T

	26	44	48
13	54	91	100
15	47	79	86
17	41	70	76
19	37	63	68
25	28	48	52
34	21	35	38

DC(HS), 43T

	28	40	48
13	58	83	100
15	50	72	86
17	44	64	76
19	40	57	68
25	30	43	52
34	22	32	38

DC, 41T

	28	42	50
13	58	87	104
15	50	76	90
17	44	67	79
19	40	60	71
25	30	45	54
34	22	33	40

DC, 43T

	24	37	46
13	50	77	96
15	43	67	83
17	38	59	73
19	34	53	65
26	25	38	48
34	19	29	37

DC, 43T

	24	39	48
13	50	81	100
15	43	70	86
17	38	62	76
19	34	55	68
26	25	41	50
34	19	31	38

DC, 45T

	24	40	48
13	50	83	100
15	43	72	86
17	38	64	76
19	34	57	68
26	25	42	50
34	19	32	38

DC, 45T

	26	39	48
13	54	81	100
15	47	70	86
17	41	62	76
19	37	55	68
26	27	41	50
34	21	31	38

DC, 43T

	26	40	48
13	54	83	100
15	47	72	86
17	41	64	76
19	37	57	68
26	27	42	50
34	21	32	38

DC, 43T

	26	44	48
13	54	91	100
15	47	79	86
17	41	70	76
19	37	63	68
26	27	46	50
34	21	35	38

DC(HS), 43T

	28	44	48
13	58	91	100
15	50	79	86
17	44	70	76
19	40	63	68
26	29	46	50
34	22	35	38

DC(HS), 41T

	28	40	50
13	58	83	104
15	50	72	90
17	44	64	79
20	38	54	68
23	33	47	59
26	29	42	52

A+"G", 35T

	26	39	48
13	54	81	100
15	47	70	86
17	41	62	76
20	35	53	65
24	29	44	54
28	25	38	46

DC(A), 37T

	26	39	50
13	54	81	104
15	47	70	90
17	41	62	79
20	35	53	68
24	29	44	56
28	25	38	48

A+G, 39T

	28	39	48
13	58	81	100
15	50	70	86
17	44	62	76
20	38	53	65
24	32	44	54
28	27	38	46

DC(A), 35T

	28	39	50
13	58	81	104
15	50	70	90
17	44	62	79
20	38	53	68
24	32	44	56
28	27	38	48

A+G, 37T

	28	42	46
13	58	87	96
15	50	76	83
17	44	67	73
20	38	57	62
24	32	47	52
28	27	41	44

HS+G, 33T

	28	44	48
13	58	91	100
15	50	79	86
17	44	70	76
20	38	59	65
24	32	50	54
28	27	42	46

HS+G, 35T

	28	46	50
13	58	96	104
15	50	83	90
17	44	73	79
20	38	62	68
24	32	52	56
28	27	44	48

HS+G, 37T

	24	39	48
13	50	81	100
15	43	70	86
17	38	62	76
20	32	53	65
24	27	44	54
30	22	35	43

DC, 41T

	24	42	46
13	50	87	96
15	43	76	83
17	38	67	73
20	32	57	62
24	27	47	52
30	22	38	41

HS+G, 39T

	24	44	48
13	50	91	100
15	43	79	86
17	38	70	76
20	32	59	65
24	27	50	54
30	22	40	43

HS+G, 41T

	26	42	46
13	54	87	96
15	47	76	83
17	41	67	73
20	35	57	62
24	29	47	52
30	23	38	41

HS+G, 37T

	26	44	48
13	54	91	100
15	47	79	86
17	41	70	76
20	35	59	65
24	29	50	54
30	23	40	43

HS+G, 39T

	28	44	48
13	58	91	100
15	50	79	86
17	44	70	76
20	38	59	65
24	32	50	54
30	25	40	43

HS+G, 37T

	24	39	48
13	50	81	100
15	43	70	86
17	38	62	76
20	32	53	65
25	26	42	52
32	20	33	41

DC, 43T

	24	42	46
13	50	87	96
15	43	76	83
17	38	67	73
20	32	57	62
25	26	45	50
32	20	35	39

HS+G, 41T

	26	42	46
13	54	87	96
15	47	76	83
17	41	67	73
20	35	57	62
25	28	45	50
32	22	35	39

HS+G, 39T

	28	44	48
13	58	91	100
15	50	79	86
17	44	70	76
20	38	59	65
25	30	48	52
32	24	37	41

HS+G, 39T

	24	38	46
13	50	79	96
15	43	68	83
17	38	60	73
20	32	51	62
25	26	41	50
34	19	30	37

DC, 43T

	24	38	48
13	50	79	100
15	43	68	86
17	38	60	76
20	32	51	65
25	26	41	52
34	19	30	38

DC, 45T

	24	39	48
13	50	81	100
15	43	70	86
17	38	62	76
20	32	53	65
25	26	42	52
34	19	31	38

DC, 45T

	24	40	48
13	50	83	100
15	43	72	86
17	38	64	76
20	32	54	65
25	26	43	52
34	19	32	38

DC, 45T

	26	38	48
13	54	79	100
15	47	68	86
17	41	60	76
20	35	51	65
25	28	41	52
34	21	30	38

DC, 43T

	26	39	48
13	54	81	100
15	47	70	86
17	41	62	76
20	35	53	65
25	28	42	52
34	21	31	38

DC, 43T

	28	40	48
13	58	83	100
15	50	72	86
17	44	64	76
20	38	54	65
25	30	43	52
34	22	32	38

DC, 41T

	24	38	46
13	50	79	96
15	43	68	83
17	38	60	73
20	32	51	62
26	25	39	48
34	19	30	37

DC, 43T

	26	38	48
13	54	79	100
15	47	68	86
17	41	60	76
20	35	51	65
26	27	39	50
34	21	30	38

DC, 43T

	26	39	48
13	54	81	100
15	47	70	86
17	41	62	76
20	35	53	65
26	27	41	50
34	21	31	38

DC, 43T

	24	38	50
13	50	79	104
15	43	68	90
18	36	57	75
21	31	49	64
25	26	41	54
30	22	34	45

A+G, 43T

	24	39	48
13	50	81	100
15	43	70	86
18	36	59	72
21	31	50	62
25	26	42	52
30	22	35	43

DC(A), 41T

	24	42	46
13	50	87	96
15	43	76	83
18	36	63	69
21	31	54	59
25	26	45	50
30	22	38	41

HS+G, 39T

	26	38	50
13	54	79	104
15	47	68	90
18	39	57	75
21	33	49	64
25	28	41	54
30	23	34	45

A+G, 41T

	28	42	46
13	58	87	96
15	50	76	83
18	42	63	69
21	36	54	59
25	30	45	50
30	25	38	41

HS+G, 35T

	28	44	48
13	58	91	100
15	50	79	86
18	42	66	72
21	36	57	62
25	30	48	52
30	25	40	43

HS+G, 37T

	28	46	50
13	58	96	104
15	50	83	90
18	42	69	75
21	36	59	64
25	30	50	54
30	25	41	45

HS+G, 39T

	30	44	48
13	62	91	100
15	54	79	86
18	45	66	72
21	39	57	62
25	32	48	52
30	27	40	43

HS+G, 35T

	30	46	50
13	62	96	104
15	54	83	90
18	45	69	75
21	39	59	64
25	32	50	54
30	27	41	45

HS+G, 37T

	24	42	46
13	50	87	96
16	41	71	78
19	34	60	65
22	29	52	56
26	25	44	48
32	20	35	39

HS+G, 41T

	28	42	46
13	58	87	96
16	47	71	78
19	40	60	65
22	34	52	56
26	29	44	48
32	24	35	39

HS+G, 37T

	28	44	48
13	58	91	100
16	47	74	81
19	40	63	68
22	34	54	59
26	29	46	50
32	24	37	41

HS+G, 39T

	28	46	50
13	58	96	104
16	47	78	84
19	40	65	71
22	34	56	61
26	29	48	52
32	24	39	42
HS+G, 41T			

	30	46	50
13	62	96	104
16	51	78	84
19	43	65	71
22	37	56	61
26	31	48	52
32	25	39	42
HS+G, 39T			

	32	46	50
13	66	96	104
16	54	78	84
19	45	65	71
22	39	56	61
26	33	48	52
32	27	39	42
HS+G, 37T			

	24	36	48
13	50	75	100
16	41	61	81
19	34	51	68
22	29	44	59
27	24	36	48
32	20	30	41
A+G, 43T			

	24	38	50
13	50	79	104
16	41	64	84
19	34	54	71
22	29	47	61
27	24	38	50
32	20	32	42
A+G, 45T			

	28	42	46
13	58	87	96
16	47	71	78
19	40	60	65
22	34	52	56
27	28	42	46
32	24	35	39
HS+G, 37T			

	28	43	48
13	58	89	100
16	47	73	81
19	40	61	68
22	34	53	59
27	28	43	48
32	24	36	41
HS+G, 39T			

	28	44	48
13	58	91	100
16	47	74	81
19	40	63	68
22	34	54	59
27	28	44	48
32	24	37	41
HS+G, 39T			

	28	45	50
13	58	93	104
16	47	76	84
19	40	64	71
22	34	55	61
27	28	45	50
32	24	38	42
HS+G, 41T			

	30	43	48
13	62	89	100
16	51	73	81
19	43	61	68
22	37	53	59
27	30	43	48
32	25	36	41
HS+G, 37T			

	30	44	48
13	62	91	100
16	51	74	81
19	43	63	68
22	37	54	59
27	30	44	48
32	25	37	41
HS+G, 37T			

	30	45	50
13	62	93	104
16	51	76	84
19	43	64	71
22	37	55	61
27	30	45	50
32	25	38	42
HS+G, 39T			

	26	41	46
13	54	85	96
16	44	69	78
19	37	58	65
22	32	50	56
27	26	41	46
34	21	33	37
HS+G, 41T			

	26	42	46
13	54	87	96
16	44	71	78
19	37	60	65
22	32	52	56
27	26	42	46
34	21	33	37
HS+G, 41T			

	28	41	46
13	58	85	96
16	47	69	78
19	40	58	65
22	34	50	56
27	28	41	46
34	22	33	37
HS+G, 39T			

	28	44	48
13	58	91	100
16	47	74	81
19	40	63	68
22	34	54	59
27	28	44	48
34	22	35	38
HS+G, 41T			

	28	43	48
13	58	89	100
16	47	73	81
19	40	61	68
23	33	50	56
28	27	41	46
34	22	34	38

HS+G, 41T

	28	45	50
13	58	93	104
16	47	76	84
19	40	64	71
23	33	53	59
28	27	43	48
34	22	36	40

HS+G, 43T

	30	45	50
13	62	93	104
16	51	76	84
19	43	64	71
23	35	53	59
28	29	43	48
34	24	36	40

HS+G, 41T

	28	40	50
14	54	77	96
16	47	68	84
18	42	60	75
21	36	51	64
24	32	45	56
28	27	39	48

A+G, 36T

	28	42	52
14	54	81	100
16	47	71	88
18	42	63	78
21	36	54	67
24	32	47	59
28	27	41	50

A+G, 38T

	28	44	52
14	54	85	100
16	47	74	88
18	42	66	78
21	36	57	67
24	32	50	59
28	27	42	50

DC, 38T

	28	45	50
14	54	87	96
16	47	76	84
18	42	68	75
21	36	58	64
24	32	51	56
28	27	43	48

C(HS), 36T

	26	40	50
14	50	77	96
16	44	68	84
18	39	60	75
21	33	51	64
26	27	42	52
34	21	32	40

DC, 44T

	28	40	50
14	54	77	96
16	47	68	84
18	42	60	75
21	36	51	64
26	29	42	52
34	22	32	40

DC, 42T

	28	42	52
14	54	81	100
16	47	71	88
18	42	63	78
21	36	54	67
26	29	44	54
34	22	33	41

DC, 44T

	24	40	51
14	46	77	98
16	41	68	86
19	34	57	72
22	29	49	63
26	25	42	53
30	22	36	46

A+G, 43T

	24	41	51
14	46	79	98
16	41	69	86
19	34	58	72
22	29	50	63
26	25	43	53
30	22	37	46

A+G, 43T

	24	42	52
14	46	81	100
16	41	71	88
19	34	60	74
22	29	52	64
26	25	44	54
30	22	38	47

A+G, 44T

	26	40	52
14	50	77	100
16	44	68	88
19	37	57	74
22	32	49	64
26	27	42	54
30	23	36	47

A+G, 42T

	28	40	50
14	54	77	96
16	47	68	84
19	40	57	71
22	34	49	61
26	29	42	52
30	25	36	45

A+G, 38T

	28	42	52
14	54	81	100
16	47	71	88
19	40	60	74
22	34	52	64
26	29	44	54
30	25	38	47

A+G, 40T

	28	46	50
14	54	89	96
16	47	78	84
19	40	65	71
22	34	56	61
26	29	48	52
30	25	41	45

HS+G, 38T

	28	48	52
14	54	93	100
16	47	81	88
19	40	68	74
22	34	59	64
26	29	50	54
30	25	43	47

HS+G, 40T

	30	46	50
14	58	89	96
16	51	78	84
19	43	65	71
22	37	56	61
26	31	48	52
30	27	41	45

HS+G, 36T

	30	48	52
14	58	93	100
16	51	81	88
19	43	68	74
22	37	59	64
26	31	50	54
30	27	43	47

HS+G, 38T

	24	38	48
14	46	73	93
16	41	64	81
19	34	54	68
22	29	47	59
26	25	39	50
32	20	32	41

DC(A), 42T

	24	40	51
14	46	77	98
16	41	68	86
19	34	57	72
22	29	49	63
26	25	42	53
32	20	34	43

DC(A), 45T

	24	41	51
14	46	79	98
16	41	69	86
19	34	58	72
22	29	50	63
26	25	43	53
32	20	35	43

DC, 45T

	26	40	50
14	50	77	96
16	44	68	84
19	37	57	71
22	32	49	61
26	27	42	52
32	22	34	42

DC, 42T

	26	41	52
14	50	79	100
16	44	69	88
19	37	58	74
22	32	50	64
26	27	43	54
32	22	35	44

DC(A), 44T

	26	42	52
14	50	81	100
16	44	71	88
19	37	60	74
22	32	52	64
26	27	44	54
32	22	35	44

DC, 44T

	28	40	52
14	54	77	100
16	47	68	88
19	40	57	74
22	34	49	64
26	29	42	54
32	24	34	44

A+G, 42T

	28	46	50
14	54	89	96
16	47	78	84
19	40	65	71
22	34	56	61
26	29	48	52
32	24	39	42

HS+G, 40T

	30	48	52
14	58	93	100
16	51	81	88
19	43	68	74
22	37	59	64
26	31	50	54
32	25	41	44

HS+G, 40T

	32	48	52
14	62	93	100
16	54	81	88
19	45	68	74
22	39	59	64
26	33	50	54
32	27	41	44

HS+G, 38T

	28	42	52
14	54	81	100
16	47	71	88
19	40	60	74
22	34	52	64
26	29	44	54
34	22	33	41

DC, 44T

	28	46	50
14	54	89	96
16	47	78	84
19	40	65	71
22	34	56	61
26	29	48	52
34	22	37	40

DC(HS), 42T

	30	48	52
14	58	93	100
16	51	81	88
19	43	68	74
22	37	59	64
26	31	50	54
34	24	38	41

DC(HS), 42T

	34	46	50
14	66	89	96
16	57	78	84
19	48	65	71
22	42	56	61
26	35	48	52
34	27	37	40

DC(HS), 36T

	34	48	52
14	66	93	100
16	57	81	88
19	48	68	74
22	42	59	64
26	35	50	54
34	27	38	41

DC(HS), 38T

	26	45	50
14	50	87	96
16	44	76	84
19	37	64	71
23	31	53	59
27	26	45	50
30	23	41	45

DC, 40T

	28	41	52
14	54	79	100
16	47	69	88
19	40	58	74
23	33	48	61
27	28	41	52
32	24	35	44

A+G, 42T

	30	46	50
14	58	89	96
16	51	78	84
19	43	65	71
23	35	54	59
27	30	46	50
32	25	39	42

HS+G, 38T

	32	48	52
14	62	93	100
16	54	81	88
19	45	68	74
23	38	56	61
27	32	48	52
32	27	41	44

HS+G, 38T

	26	42	46
14	50	81	89
16	44	71	78
19	37	60	65
23	31	49	54
28	25	41	44
32	22	35	39

HS+G, 38T

	28	46	50
14	54	89	96
17	44	73	79
20	38	62	68
24	32	52	56
27	28	46	50
34	22	37	40

HS+G, 42T

	30	48	52
14	58	93	100
17	48	76	83
20	41	65	70
24	34	54	59
27	30	48	52
34	24	38	41

HS+G, 42T

	28	40	52
14	54	77	100
17	44	64	83
20	38	54	70
24	32	45	59
28	27	39	50
34	22	32	41

A+G, 44T

	28	44	50
14	54	85	96
17	44	70	79
20	38	59	68
24	32	50	56
28	27	42	48
34	22	35	40

DC(HS), 42T

	28	46	50
14	54	89	96
17	44	73	79
20	38	62	68
24	32	52	56
28	27	44	48
34	22	37	40

HS+G, 42T

	30	46	50
14	58	89	96
17	48	73	79
20	41	62	68
24	34	52	56
28	29	44	48
34	24	37	40

HS+G, 40T

	30	48	52
14	58	93	100
17	48	76	83
20	41	65	70
24	34	54	59
28	29	46	50
34	24	38	41

HS+G, 42T

	28	45	50
14	54	87	96
17	44	71	79
21	36	58	64
24	32	51	56
28	27	43	48
34	22	36	40

HS+G, 42T

E: 10-SPEED GEARINGS 26-INCH WHEELS

	44	48
13	88	96
15	76	83
18	64	69
22	52	57
30	38	42

C(HS), 21T

	30	48
13	60	96
15	52	83
18	43	69
24	33	52
32	24	39

WS, 37T

	43	48
13	86	96
16	70	78
19	59	66
24	47	52
32	35	39

C(HS), 24T

	45	50
13	90	100
16	73	81
19	62	68
24	49	54
32	37	41

C(HS), 24T

	36	48
13	72	96
16	59	78
20	47	62
24	39	52
30	31	42

A, 29T

	43	48
13	86	96
16	70	78
20	56	62
24	47	52
30	37	42

HS, 22T

	40	48
13	80	96
16	65	78
20	52	62
25	42	50
32	33	39

C(HS), 27T

	43	48
13	86	96
16	70	78
20	56	62
25	45	50
32	35	39

HS, 24T

	43	48
13	86	96
16	70	78
20	56	62
26	43	48
34	33	37

HS, 26T

	36	52
14	67	97
15	62	90
17	55	80
20	47	68
26	36	52

WS, 28T

	46	50
14	85	93
16	75	81
19	63	68
22	54	59
30	40	43

C(HS), 20T

	48	52
14	89	97
16	78	85
19	66	71
22	57	61
30	42	45

C(HS), 20T

	34	52
14	63	97
16	55	85
19	47	71
23	38	59
28	32	48

WS, 32T

	42	52
14	78	97
16	68	85
19	57	71
23	47	59
30	36	45

C, 26T

	42	52
14	78	97
16	68	85
19	57	71
24	46	56
28	39	48

C, 24T

	32	52
14	59	97
16	52	85
19	44	71
24	35	56
32	26	42

WS, 38T

	42	52
14	78	97
16	68	85
19	57	71
24	46	56
32	34	42

C, 28T

	30	52
14	56	97
16	49	85
19	41	71
25	31	54
34	23	40

WS, 42T

	40	50
14	74	93
16	65	81
19	55	68
25	42	52
34	31	38

C, 30T

	42	52
14	78	97
16	68	85
19	57	71
25	44	54
34	32	40

C, 30T

	39	50
14	72	93
17	60	76
20	51	65
24	42	54
28	36	46

A, 25T

	40	50
14	74	93
17	61	76
20	52	65
24	43	54
28	37	46

C(A), 24T

	40	51
14	74	95
17	61	78
20	52	66
24	43	55
28	37	47

A, 25T

	40	52
14	74	97
17	61	80
20	52	68
24	43	56
28	37	48

A, 26T

	42	52
14	78	97
17	64	80
20	55	68
24	46	56
28	39	48

C(A), 24T

	45	50
14	84	93
17	69	76
20	59	65
24	49	54
28	42	46

HS, 19T

	39	52
14	72	97
17	60	80
20	51	68
24	42	56
30	34	45

A, 29T

	47	52
14	87	97
17	72	80
20	61	68
24	51	56
30	41	45

HS, 21T

	38	52
14	71	97
17	58	80
21	47	64
26	38	52
32	31	42

A, 32T

	43	48
14	80	89
17	66	73
21	53	59
26	43	48
32	35	39

HS, 23T

	45	50
14	84	93
17	69	76
21	56	62
26	45	50
32	37	41

HS, 23T

	47	52
14	87	97
17	72	80
21	58	64
26	47	52
32	38	42

HS, 23T

	44	50
14	82	93
17	67	76
21	54	62
26	44	50
34	34	38

HS, 26T

	45	50
14	84	93
17	69	76
21	56	62
26	45	50
34	34	38

HS, 25T

	48	52
14	89	97
17	73	80
21	59	64
26	48	52
34	37	40

HS, 24T

F: 12-SPEED GEARINGS 26-INCH WHEELS

	38	46
13	76	92
15	66	80
17	58	70
19	52	63
25	40	48
32	31	37

C, 27T

	39	48
13	78	96
15	68	83
17	60	73
19	53	66
25	41	50
32	32	39

C, 28T

	40	48
13	80	96
15	69	83
17	61	73
19	55	66
25	42	50
32	33	39

C, 27T

	42	50
13	84	100
15	73	87
17	64	76
19	57	68
25	44	52
32	34	41

C, 27T

	37	46
13	74	92
15	64	80
17	57	70
19	51	63
25	38	48
34	28	35

C, 30T

	38	46
13	76	92
15	66	80
17	58	70
19	52	63
25	40	48
34	29	35

C, 29T

	39	48
13	78	96
15	68	83
17	60	73
19	53	66
25	41	50
34	30	37

C, 30T

	40	48
13	80	96
15	69	83
17	61	73
19	55	66
25	42	50
34	31	37

C, 29T

	42	50
13	84	100
15	73	87
17	64	76
19	57	68
25	44	52
34	32	38

C, 29T

	44	48
13	88	96
15	76	83
17	67	73
19	60	66
25	46	50
34	34	37

C(HS), 25T

	37	46
13	74	92
15	64	80
17	57	70
19	51	63
26	37	46
34	28	35

C, 30T

	39	48
13	78	96
15	68	83
17	60	73
19	53	66
26	39	48
34	30	37

C, 30T

	40	48
13	80	96
15	69	83
17	61	73
19	55	66
26	40	48
34	31	37

C, 29T

	44	48
13	88	96
15	76	83
17	67	73
19	60	66
26	44	48
34	34	37

C(HS), 25T

	39	48
13	78	96
15	68	83
17	60	73
20	51	62
24	42	52
28	36	45

C(A), 24T

	42	46
13	84	92
15	73	80
17	64	70
20	55	60
24	46	50
28	39	43

HS, 19T

	44	48
13	88	96
15	76	83
17	67	73
20	57	62
24	48	52
28	41	45

HS, 19T

	46	50
13	92	100
15	80	87
17	70	76
20	60	65
24	50	54
28	43	46

HS, 19T

	30	48
13	60	96
15	52	83
17	46	73
20	39	62
25	31	50
34	23	37

WS, 39T

	38	48
13	76	96
15	66	83
17	58	73
20	49	62
25	40	50
34	29	37

C, 31T

	38	50
13	76	100
15	66	87
18	55	72
21	47	62
25	40	52
30	33	43

A, 29T

	39	48
13	78	96
15	68	83
18	56	69
21	48	59
25	41	50
30	34	42

C(A), 26T

	44	48
13	88	96
15	76	83
18	64	69
21	54	59
25	46	50
30	38	42

HS, 21T

	46	50
13	92	100
15	80	87
18	66	72
21	57	62
25	48	52
30	40	43

HS, 21T

	40	50
13	80	100
16	65	81
19	55	68
22	47	59
26	40	50
32	33	41

C(A), 29T

	42	46
13	84	92
16	68	75
19	57	63
22	50	54
26	42	46
32	34	37

HS, 23T

	42	52
13	84	104
16	68	85
19	57	71
22	50	61
26	42	52
32	34	42

C, 29T

	44	48
13	88	96
16	72	78
19	60	66
22	52	57
26	44	48
32	36	39

HS, 23T

	46	50
13	92	100
16	75	81
19	63	68
22	54	59
26	46	50
32	37	41

HS, 23T

	42	46
13	84	92
16	68	75
19	57	63
22	50	54
27	40	44
32	34	37

HS, 23T

	44	48
13	88	96
16	72	78
19	60	66
22	52	57
27	42	46
32	36	39

HS, 23T

	42	46
13	84	92
16	68	75
19	57	63
22	50	54
27	40	44
34	32	35

HS, 25T

	44	48
13	88	96
16	72	78
19	60	66
22	52	57
27	42	46
34	34	37

HS, 25T

	43	48
13	86	96
16	70	78
19	59	66
23	49	54
28	40	45
34	33	37

HS, 26T

	45	50
13	90	100
16	73	81
19	62	68
23	51	57
28	42	46
34	34	38

HS, 26T

	34	52
14	63	97
15	59	90
17	52	80
20	44	68
23	38	59
28	32	48

WS, 32T

	32	52
14	59	97
15	55	90
17	49	80
20	42	68
25	33	54
32	26	42

WS, 38T

	34	52
14	63	97
15	59	90
17	52	80
20	44	68
26	34	52
34	26	40

WS, 38T

	38	50
14	71	93
16	62	81
18	55	72
20	49	65
23	43	57
26	38	50

C, 24T

	34	52
14	63	97
16	55	85
18	49	75
21	42	64
26	34	52
32	28	42

WS, 36T

	40	50
14	74	93
16	65	81
18	58	72
21	50	62
26	40	50
34	31	38
C, 30T		

	42	52
14	78	97
16	68	85
18	61	75
21	52	64
26	42	52
34	32	40
C, 30T		

	40	52
14	74	97
16	65	85
19	55	71
22	47	61
26	40	52
30	35	45
A, 28T		

	40	50
14	74	93
16	65	81
19	55	68
22	47	59
26	40	50
32	33	41
C(A), 28T		

	42	52
14	78	97
16	68	85
19	57	71
22	50	61
26	42	52
32	34	42
C, 28T		

	46	50
14	85	93
16	75	81
19	63	68
22	54	59
26	46	50
32	37	41
HS, 22T		

	48	52
14	89	97
16	78	85
19	66	71
22	57	61
26	48	52
32	39	42
HS, 22T		

	32	52
14	59	97
16	52	85
19	44	71
22	38	61
26	32	52
34	24	40
WS, 40T		

	42	52
14	78	97
16	68	85
19	57	71
22	50	61
26	42	52
34	32	40
C, 30T		

	46	50
14	85	93
16	75	81
19	63	68
22	54	59
26	46	50
34	35	38
C(HS), 24T		

	48	52
14	89	97
16	78	85
19	66	71
22	57	61
26	48	52
34	37	40
C(HS), 24T		

	46	50
14	85	93
16	75	81
19	63	68
23	52	57
27	44	48
32	37	41
HS, 22T		

	46	50
14	85	93
17	70	76
20	60	65
24	50	54
27	44	48
34	35	38
HS, 24T		

	48	52
14	89	97
17	73	80
20	62	68
24	52	56
27	46	50
34	37	40
HS, 24T		

	39	52
14	72	97
17	60	80
20	51	68
24	42	56
28	36	48
32	32	42
C, 31T		

	40	52
14	74	97
17	61	80
20	52	68
24	43	56
28	37	48
34	31	40
A, 32T		

	42	52
14	78	97
17	64	80
20	55	68
24	46	56
28	39	48
34	32	40
C(A), 30T		

	45	50
14	84	93
17	69	76
20	59	65
24	49	54
28	42	46
34	34	38
HS, 25T		

	46	50
14	85	93
17	70	76
20	60	65
24	50	54
28	43	46
34	35	38
HS, 24T		

	48	52
14	89	97
17	73	80
20	62	68
24	52	56
28	45	48
34	37	40
HS, 24T		

G: 15-SPEED GEARINGS 26-INCH WHEELS

	24	38	46
13	48	76	92
15	42	66	80
18	35	55	66
22	28	45	54
30	21	33	40

DC, 39T

	24	40	48
13	48	80	96
15	42	69	83
18	35	58	69
22	28	47	57
30	21	35	42

DC, 41T

	24	42	46
13	48	84	92
15	42	73	80
18	35	61	66
22	28	50	54
30	21	36	40

DC(HS), 39T

	24	44	48
13	48	88	96
15	42	76	83
18	35	64	69
22	28	52	57
30	21	38	42

DC(HS), 41T

	28	44	48
13	56	88	96
15	49	76	83
18	40	64	69
22	33	52	57
30	24	38	42

DC(HS), 37T

	26	42	46
13	52	84	92
16	42	68	75
19	36	57	63
23	29	47	52
28	24	39	43

HS+G, 35T

	26	43	48
13	52	86	96
16	42	70	78
19	36	59	66
23	29	49	54
28	24	40	45

HS+G, 37T

	26	44	48
13	52	88	96
16	42	72	78
19	36	60	66
23	29	50	54
28	24	41	45

HS+G, 37T

	26	45	50
13	52	90	100
16	42	73	81
19	36	62	68
23	29	51	57
28	24	42	46

HS+G, 39T

	28	44	48
13	56	88	96
16	46	72	78
19	38	60	66
23	32	50	54
28	26	41	45

HS+G, 35T

	28	46	50
13	56	92	100
16	46	75	81
19	38	63	68
23	32	52	57
28	26	43	46

HS+G, 37T

	24	41	46
13	48	82	92
16	39	67	75
19	33	56	63
24	26	44	50
32	20	33	37

DC(HS), 41T

	24	42	46
13	48	84	92
16	39	68	75
19	33	57	63
24	26	46	50
32	20	34	37

DC(HS), 41T

	24	43	48
13	48	86	96
16	39	70	78
19	33	59	66
24	26	47	52
32	20	35	39

DC(HS), 43T

	24	44	48
13	48	88	96
16	39	72	78
19	33	60	66
24	26	48	52
32	20	36	39

DC(HS), 43T

	26	45	50
13	52	90	100
16	42	73	81
19	36	62	68
24	28	49	54
32	21	37	41

DC(HS), 43T

	28	38	48
13	56	76	96
16	46	62	78
20	36	49	62
24	30	41	52
28	26	35	45

DC, 35T

	24	34	46
13	48	68	92
16	39	55	75
20	31	44	60
24	26	37	50
30	21	29	40

A+G, 39T

	24	41	46
13	48	82	92
16	39	67	75
20	31	53	60
24	26	44	50
30	21	36	40

HS+G, 39T

	28	43	48
13	56	86	96
16	46	70	78
20	36	56	62
24	30	47	52
30	24	37	42

HS+G, 37T

	24	40	48
13	48	80	96
16	39	65	78
20	31	52	62
25	25	42	50
32	20	33	39

DC(HS), 43T

	26	41	46
13	52	82	92
16	42	67	75
20	34	53	60
25	27	43	48
32	21	33	37

HS+G, 39T

	28	43	48
13	56	86	96
16	46	70	78
20	36	56	62
25	29	45	50
32	23	35	39

HS+G, 39T

	28	45	50
13	56	90	100
16	46	73	81
20	36	59	65
25	29	47	52
32	23	37	41

HS+G, 41T

	24	36	46
13	48	72	92
16	39	59	75
20	31	47	60
26	24	36	46
34	18	28	35

DC, 43T

	24	41	46
13	48	82	92
16	39	67	75
20	31	53	60
26	24	41	46
34	18	31	35

HS+G, 43T

	26	43	48
13	52	86	96
16	42	70	78
20	34	56	62
26	26	43	48
34	20	33	37

HS+G, 43T

	28	45	50
13	56	90	100
16	46	73	81
20	36	59	65
26	28	45	50
34	21	34	38

HS+G, 43T

	28	38	48
14	52	71	89
16	46	62	78
19	38	52	66
22	33	45	57
26	28	38	48

A+"G", 32T

	24	46	50
14	45	85	93
16	39	75	81
19	33	63	68
22	28	54	59
30	21	40	43

DC(HS), 42T

	28	46	50
14	52	85	93
16	46	75	81
19	38	63	68
22	33	54	59
30	24	40	43

DC(HS), 38T

	28	48	52
14	52	89	97
16	46	78	85
19	38	66	71
22	33	57	61
30	24	42	45

DC(HS), 40T

	28	42	52
14	52	78	97
16	46	68	85
19	38	57	71
23	32	47	59
28	26	39	48

DC(A), 38T

	28	46	50
14	52	85	93
16	46	75	81
19	38	63	68
23	32	52	57
28	26	43	46

HS+G, 36T

	24	40	50
14	45	74	93
16	39	65	81
19	33	55	68
23	27	45	57
30	21	35	43

DC, 42T

	26	42	52
14	48	78	97
16	42	68	85
19	36	57	71
23	29	47	59
30	23	36	45

DC, 42T

	24	38	48
14	45	71	89
16	39	62	78
19	33	52	66
24	26	41	52
28	22	35	45

DC, 38T

	28	40	50
14	52	74	93
16	46	65	81
19	38	55	68
24	30	43	54
28	26	37	46

DC, 36T

	28	42	52
14	52	78	97
16	46	68	85
19	38	57	71
24	30	46	56
28	26	39	48

DC, 38T

	24	40	50
14	45	74	93
16	39	65	81
19	33	55	68
24	26	43	54
32	20	33	41

DC, 44T

	28	42	52
14	52	78	97
16	46	68	85
19	38	57	71
24	30	46	56
32	23	34	42

DC, 42T

	24	37	50
14	45	69	93
17	37	57	76
20	31	48	65
24	26	40	54
28	22	34	46

A+G, 40T

	24	39	50
14	45	72	93
17	37	60	76
20	31	51	65
24	26	42	54
28	22	36	46

A+G, 40T

	24	40	50
14	45	74	93
17	37	61	76
20	31	52	65
24	26	43	54
28	22	37	46

DC(A), 40T

	24	40	52
14	45	74	97
17	37	61	80
20	31	52	68
24	26	43	56
28	22	37	48

A+G, 42T

	24	42	52
14	45	78	97
17	37	64	80
20	31	55	68
24	26	46	56
28	22	39	48

DC(A), 42T

	24	45	50
14	45	84	93
17	37	69	76
20	31	59	65
24	26	49	54
28	22	42	46

HS+G, 40T

	24	46	50
14	45	85	93
17	37	70	76
20	31	60	65
24	26	50	54
28	22	43	46

HS+G, 40T

	26	36	46
14	48	67	85
17	40	55	70
20	34	47	60
24	28	39	50
28	24	33	43

A+G, 34T

	26	40	52
14	48	74	97
17	40	61	80
20	34	52	68
24	28	43	56
28	24	37	48

A+G, 40T

	28	38	48
14	52	71	89
17	43	58	73
20	36	49	62
24	30	41	52
28	26	35	45

A+G, 34T

	28	39	50
14	52	72	93
17	43	60	76
20	36	51	65
24	30	42	54
28	26	36	46

A+G, 36T

	28	39	52
14	52	72	97
17	43	60	80
20	36	51	68
24	30	42	56
28	26	36	48

A+G, 38T

	28	40	50
14	52	74	93
17	43	61	76
20	36	52	65
24	30	43	54
28	26	37	46

DC(A), 36T

	28	40	52
14	52	74	97
17	43	61	80
20	36	52	68
24	30	43	56
28	26	37	48

A+G, 38T

	28	42	52
14	52	78	97
17	43	64	80
20	36	55	68
24	30	46	56
28	26	39	48

DC(A), 38T

	28	45	50
14	52	84	93
17	43	69	76
20	36	59	65
24	30	49	54
28	26	42	46

HS+G, 36T

	28	45	52
14	52	84	97
17	43	69	80
20	36	59	68
24	30	49	56
28	26	42	48

DC(HS), 38T

	28	46	50
14	52	85	93
17	43	70	76
20	36	60	65
24	30	50	54
28	26	43	46

HS+G, 36T

	28	47	52
14	52	87	97
17	43	72	80
20	36	61	68
24	30	51	56
28	26	44	48

HS+G, 38T

	28	48	52
14	52	89	97
17	43	73	80
20	36	62	68
24	30	52	56
28	26	45	48

HS+G, 38T

	24	39	52
14	45	72	97
17	37	60	80
20	31	51	68
24	26	42	56
30	21	34	45

A+G, 44T

	28	45	50
14	52	84	93
17	43	69	76
20	36	59	65
24	30	49	54
30	24	39	43

HS+G, 38T

	28	47	52
14	52	87	97
17	43	72	80
20	36	61	68
24	30	51	56
30	24	41	45

HS+G, 40T

	28	36	48
14	52	67	89
17	43	55	73
20	36	47	62
26	28	36	48
32	23	29	39

DC(A), 38T

	24	43	48
14	45	80	89
17	37	66	73
21	30	53	59
26	24	43	48
32	20	35	39

HS+G, 42T

	24	45	50
14	45	84	93
17	37	69	76
21	30	56	62
26	24	45	50
32	20	37	41

HS+G, 44T

	26	45	50
14	48	84	93
17	40	69	76
21	32	56	62
26	26	45	50
32	21	37	41

HS+G, 42T

	28	43	48
14	52	80	89
17	43	66	73
21	35	53	59
26	28	43	48
32	23	35	39

HS+G, 38T

	28	45	50
14	52	84	93
17	43	69	76
21	35	56	62
26	28	45	50
32	23	37	41

HS+G, 40T

	28	47	52
14	52	87	97
17	43	72	80
21	35	58	64
26	28	47	52
32	23	38	42

HS+G, 42T

	26	38	50
14	48	71	93
17	40	58	76
21	32	47	62
26	26	38	50
34	20	29	38

DC, 44T

	26	43	48
14	48	80	89
17	40	66	73
21	32	53	59
26	26	43	48
34	20	33	37

HS+G, 42T

	26	45	50
14	48	84	93
17	40	69	76
21	32	56	62
26	26	45	50
34	20	34	38

HS+G, 44T

	28	44	50
14	52	82	93
17	43	67	76
21	35	54	62
26	28	44	50
34	21	34	38

HS+G, 42T

	28	45	50
14	52	84	93
17	43	69	76
21	35	56	62
26	28	45	50
34	21	34	38

HS+G, 42T

	28	46	50
14	52	85	93
17	43	70	76
21	35	57	62
26	28	46	50
34	21	35	38

DC(HS), 42T

	28	47	52
14	52	87	97
17	43	72	80
21	35	58	64
26	28	47	52
34	21	36	40

HS+G, 44T

	26	36	46
14	48	67	85
17	40	55	70
22	31	43	54
26	26	36	46
32	21	29	37

DC, 38T

	34	40	48
14	63	74	89
17	52	61	73
22	40	47	57
28	32	37	45
34	26	31	37

DC, 34T

H: 18-SPEED GEARINGS 26-INCH WHEELS

	24	38	46
13	48	76	92
15	42	66	80
17	37	58	70
19	33	52	63
25	25	40	48
32	20	31	37

DC, 41T

	24	39	48
13	48	78	96
15	42	68	83
17	37	60	73
19	33	52	66
25	25	41	50
32	20	32	39

DC, 43T

	24	40	48
13	48	80	96
15	42	69	83
17	37	61	73
19	33	55	66
25	25	42	50
32	20	33	39

DC, 43T

	24	42	50
13	48	84	100
15	42	73	87
17	37	64	76
19	33	57	68
25	25	44	52
32	20	34	41

DC, 45T

	26	42	50
13	52	84	100
15	45	73	87
17	40	64	76
19	36	57	68
25	27	44	52
32	21	34	41

DC, 43T

	24	38	46
13	48	76	92
15	42	66	80
17	37	58	70
19	33	52	63
25	25	40	48
34	18	29	35

DC, 43T

	24	39	48
13	48	78	96
15	42	66	83
17	37	60	73
19	33	53	66
25	25	41	50
34	18	30	37

DC, 45T

	24	40	48
13	48	80	96
15	42	69	83
17	37	61	73
19	33	55	66
25	25	42	50
34	18	31	37

DC, 45T

	24	44	48
13	48	88	96
15	42	76	83
17	37	67	73
19	33	60	66
25	25	46	50
34	18	34	37

DC(HS), 45T

	26	40	48
13	52	80	96
15	45	69	83
17	40	61	73
19	36	55	66
25	27	42	50
34	20	31	37

DC, 43T

	26	44	48
13	52	88	96
15	45	76	83
17	40	67	73
19	36	60	66
25	27	46	50
34	20	34	37

DC(HS), 43T

	24	37	46
13	48	74	92
15	42	64	80
17	37	57	70
19	33	51	63
26	24	37	46
34	18	28	35

DC, 43T

	24	39	48
13	48	78	96
15	42	68	83
17	37	60	73
19	33	53	66
26	24	39	48
34	18	30	37

DC, 45T

	24	40	48
13	48	80	96
15	42	69	83
17	37	61	73
19	33	55	66
26	24	40	48
34	18	31	37

DC, 45T

	26	39	48
13	52	78	96
15	45	68	83
17	40	60	73
19	36	53	66
26	26	39	48
34	20	30	37

DC, 43T

	26	40	48
13	52	80	96
15	45	69	83
17	40	61	73
19	36	55	66
26	26	40	48
34	20	31	37

DC, 43T

H: 18-SPEED GEARINGS, 26-INCH WHEELS

	26	44	48
13	52	88	96
15	45	76	83
17	40	67	73
19	36	60	66
26	26	44	48
34	20	34	37

DC(HS), 43T

	28	44	48
13	56	88	96
15	49	76	83
17	43	67	73
19	38	60	66
26	28	44	48
34	21	34	37

DC(HS), 41T

	28	40	50
13	56	80	100
15	49	69	87
17	43	61	76
20	36	52	65
23	32	45	57
26	28	40	50

A+"G", 35T

	26	36	46
13	52	72	92
15	45	62	80
17	40	55	70
20	34	47	60
24	28	39	50
28	24	33	43

DC(A), 35T

	28	38	48
13	56	76	96
15	49	66	83
17	43	58	73
20	36	49	62
24	30	41	52
28	26	35	45

A+G, 35T

	28	39	48
13	56	78	96
15	49	68	83
17	43	60	73
20	36	51	62
24	30	42	52
28	26	36	45

DC(A), 35T

	28	39	50
13	56	78	100
15	49	68	87
17	43	60	76
20	36	51	65
24	30	42	54
28	26	36	46

A+G, 37T

	28	42	46
13	56	84	92
15	49	73	80
17	43	64	70
20	36	55	60
24	30	46	50
28	26	39	43

HS+G, 33T

	28	44	48
13	56	88	96
15	49	76	83
17	43	67	73
20	36	57	62
24	30	48	52
28	26	41	45

HS+G, 35T

	28	46	50
13	56	92	100
15	49	80	87
17	43	70	76
20	36	60	65
24	30	50	54
28	26	43	46

HS+G, 37T

	24	38	48
13	48	76	96
15	42	66	83
17	37	58	73
20	31	49	62
24	26	41	52
30	21	33	42

DC(A), 41T

	24	39	48
13	48	78	96
15	42	68	83
17	37	60	73
20	31	51	62
24	26	42	52
30	21	34	42

DC, 41T

	24	42	46
13	48	84	92
15	42	73	80
17	37	64	70
20	31	55	60
24	26	46	50
30	21	36	40

HS+G, 39T

	26	42	46
13	52	84	92
15	45	73	80
17	40	64	70
20	34	55	60
24	28	46	50
30	23	36	40

HS+G, 37T

	26	44	48
13	52	88	96
15	45	76	83
17	40	67	73
20	34	57	62
24	28	48	52
30	23	38	42

HS+G, 39T

	28	42	46
13	56	84	92
15	49	73	80
17	43	64	70
20	36	55	60
24	30	46	50
28	24	36	40

HS+G, 35T

	24	39	48
13	48	78	96
15	42	68	83
17	37	60	73
20	31	51	62
25	25	41	50
32	20	32	39

DC, 43T

	24	42	46
13	48	84	92
15	42	73	80
17	37	64	70
20	31	55	60
25	25	44	48
32	20	34	37

HS+G, 41T

	26	42	46
13	52	84	92
15	45	73	80
17	40	64	70
20	34	55	60
25	27	44	48
32	21	34	37

HS+G, 39T

	26	44	48
13	52	88	96
15	45	76	83
17	40	67	73
20	34	57	62
25	27	46	50
32	21	36	39

HS+G, 41T

	28	42	46
13	56	84	92
15	49	73	80
17	43	64	70
20	36	55	60
25	29	44	48
32	23	34	37

HS+G, 37T

	28	44	48
13	56	88	96
15	49	76	83
17	43	67	73
20	36	57	62
25	29	46	50
32	23	36	39

HS+G, 39T

	24	36	46
13	48	72	92
15	42	62	80
17	37	55	70
20	31	47	60
25	25	37	48
34	18	28	35

DC, 43T

	24	38	46
13	48	76	92
15	42	66	80
17	37	58	70
20	31	49	60
25	25	40	48
34	18	29	35

DC, 43T

	26	38	48
13	52	76	96
15	45	66	83
17	40	58	73
20	34	49	62
25	27	40	50
34	20	29	37

DC, 43T

	26	39	48
13	52	78	96
15	45	68	83
17	40	60	73
20	34	51	62
25	27	41	50
34	20	30	37

DC, 43T

	28	44	48
13	56	88	96
15	49	76	83
17	43	67	73
20	36	57	62
26	28	44	48
32	23	36	39

DC(HS), 39T

	24	38	46
13	48	76	92
15	42	66	80
17	37	58	70
20	31	49	60
26	24	38	46
34	18	29	35

DC, 43T

	26	38	48
13	52	76	96
15	45	66	83
17	40	58	73
20	34	49	62
26	26	38	48
34	20	29	37

DC, 43T

	26	39	48
13	52	78	96
15	45	68	83
17	40	60	73
20	34	51	62
26	26	39	48
34	20	30	37

DC, 43T

	26	36	46
13	52	72	92
15	45	62	80
17	40	55	70
21	32	45	57
24	28	39	50
30	23	31	40

DC(A), 37T

	28	38	48
13	56	76	96
15	49	66	83
17	43	58	73
21	35	47	59
26	28	38	48
32	23	31	39

DC(A), 39T

	24	38	50
13	48	76	100
15	42	66	87
18	35	55	72
21	30	47	62
25	25	40	52
30	21	33	43

A+G, 43T

	24	39	48
13	48	78	96
15	42	68	83
18	35	56	69
21	30	48	59
25	25	41	50
30	21	34	42

DC(A), 41T

	24	42	46
13	48	84	92
15	42	73	80
18	35	61	66
21	30	52	57
25	25	44	48
30	21	36	40

HS+G, 39T

	28	38	48
13	56	76	96
15	49	66	83
18	40	55	69
21	35	47	59
25	29	40	50
30	24	33	42

A+G, 37T

	28	42	46
13	56	84	92
15	49	73	80
18	40	61	66
21	35	52	57
25	29	44	48
30	24	36	40

HS+G, 35T

	28	44	48
13	56	88	96
15	49	76	83
18	40	64	69
21	35	54	59
25	29	46	50
30	24	38	42

HS+G, 37T

	30	46	50
13	60	92	100
15	52	80	87
18	43	66	72
21	37	57	62
25	31	48	52
30	26	40	43

HS+G, 37T

	26	36	46
13	52	72	92
16	42	59	75
17	40	55	70
21	32	45	57
24	28	39	50
30	23	31	40

DC(A), 37T

	24	36	48
13	48	72	96
16	39	59	78
19	33	49	66
22	28	43	57
26	24	36	48
32	20	29	39

A+G, 43T

	26	36	46
13	52	72	92
16	42	59	75
19	36	49	63
22	31	43	54
26	26	36	46
32	21	29	37

DC(A), 39T

	26	42	46
13	52	84	92
16	42	68	75
19	36	57	63
22	31	50	54
26	26	42	46
32	21	34	37

HS+G, 39T

	28	44	48
13	56	88	96
16	46	72	78
19	38	60	66
22	33	52	57
26	28	44	48
32	23	36	39

HS+G, 39T

	30	46	50
13	60	92	100
16	49	75	81
19	41	63	68
22	35	54	59
26	30	46	50
32	24	37	41

HS+G, 39T

	24	42	46
13	48	84	92
16	39	68	75
19	33	57	63
22	28	50	54
27	23	40	44
32	20	34	37

HS+G, 41T

	28	43	48
13	56	86	96
16	46	70	78
19	38	59	66
22	33	51	57
27	27	41	46
32	23	35	39

HS+G, 39T

	28	44	48
13	56	88	96
16	46	72	78
19	38	60	66
22	33	52	57
27	27	42	46
32	23	36	39

HS+G, 39T

H: 18-SPEED GEARINGS, 26-INCH WHEELS

	30	45	50
13	60	90	100
16	49	73	81
19	41	62	68
22	35	53	59
27	29	43	48
32	24	37	41

HS+G, 39T

	24	38	48
13	48	76	96
16	39	62	78
19	33	52	66
22	28	45	57
27	23	37	46
34	18	29	37

DC, 45T

	26	42	46
13	52	84	92
16	42	68	75
19	36	57	63
22	31	50	54
27	25	40	44
34	20	32	35

HS+G, 41T

	28	44	48
13	56	88	96
16	46	72	78
19	38	60	66
22	33	52	57
27	27	42	46
34	21	34	37

HS+G, 41T

	30	45	50
13	60	90	100
16	49	73	81
19	41	62	68
22	35	53	59
27	29	43	48
34	23	34	38

HS+G, 41T

	28	43	48
13	56	86	96
16	46	70	78
19	38	59	66
23	32	49	54
28	26	40	45
34	21	33	37

HS+G, 41T

	28	45	50
13	56	90	100
16	46	73	81
19	38	62	68
23	32	51	57
28	26	42	46
34	21	34	38

HS+G, 43T

	28	38	48
14	52	71	89
15	49	66	83
17	43	58	73
21	35	47	59
25	29	40	50
30	24	33	42

DC, 36T

	28	38	48
14	52	71	89
15	49	66	83
17	43	58	73
21	35	47	59
26	28	38	48
32	23	31	39

DC, 38T

	28	40	48
14	52	74	89
15	49	69	83
17	43	61	73
21	35	50	59
26	28	40	48
32	23	33	39

DC, 38T

	26	40	50
14	48	74	93
16	42	65	81
18	38	58	72
21	32	50	62
24	28	43	54
28	24	37	46

A+G, 38T

	28	42	52
14	52	78	97
16	46	68	85
18	40	61	75
21	35	52	64
24	30	46	56
28	26	39	48

A+G, 38T

	26	36	46
14	48	67	85
16	42	59	75
18	38	52	66
21	32	45	57
24	28	39	50
30	23	31	40

A+G, 36T

	28	38	48
14	52	71	89
16	46	62	78
18	40	55	69
21	35	47	59
24	30	41	52
30	24	33	42

A+G, 36T

	26	40	50
14	48	74	93
16	42	65	81
18	38	58	72
21	32	50	62
26	26	40	50
34	20	31	38

DC, 44T

	28	42	52
14	52	78	97
16	46	68	85
18	40	61	75
21	35	52	64
26	28	42	52
34	21	32	40

DC, 44T

	24	40	52
14	45	74	97
16	39	65	85
19	33	55	71
22	28	47	61
26	24	40	52
30	21	35	45

A+G, 44T

	24	42	52
14	45	78	97
16	39	68	85
19	33	57	71
22	28	50	61
26	24	42	52
30	21	36	45

A+G, 44T

	26	40	52
14	48	74	97
16	42	65	85
19	36	55	71
22	31	47	61
26	26	40	52
30	23	35	45

A+G, 42T

	28	40	50
14	52	74	93
16	46	65	81
19	38	55	68
22	33	47	59
26	28	40	50
30	24	35	43

A+G, 38T

	28	42	52
14	52	78	97
16	46	68	85
19	38	57	71
22	33	50	61
26	28	42	52
30	24	36	45

A+G, 40T

	28	46	50
14	52	85	93
16	46	75	81
19	38	63	68
22	33	54	59
26	28	46	50
30	24	40	43

HS+G, 38T

	28	48	52
14	52	89	97
16	46	78	85
19	38	66	71
22	33	57	61
26	28	48	52
30	24	42	45

HS+G, 40T

	30	46	50
14	56	85	93
16	49	75	81
19	41	63	68
22	35	54	59
26	30	46	50
30	26	40	43

HS+G, 36T

	30	48	52
14	56	89	97
16	49	78	85
19	41	66	71
22	35	57	61
26	30	48	52
30	26	42	45

HS+G, 38T

	24	38	48
14	45	71	89
16	39	62	78
19	33	52	66
22	28	45	57
26	24	38	48
32	20	31	39

DC(A), 42T

	26	40	50
14	48	74	93
16	42	65	81
19	36	55	68
22	31	47	59
26	26	40	50
32	21	33	41

DC(A), 42T

	26	42	52
14	48	78	97
16	42	68	85
19	36	57	71
22	31	50	61
26	26	42	52
32	21	34	42

DC, 44T

	28	46	50
14	52	85	93
16	46	75	81
19	38	63	68
22	33	54	59
26	28	46	50
32	23	37	41

HS+G, 40T

	30	48	52
14	56	89	97
16	49	78	85
19	41	66	71
22	35	57	61
26	30	48	52
32	24	39	42

HS+G, 40T

	32	48	52
14	59	89	97
16	52	78	85
19	44	66	71
22	38	57	61
26	32	48	52
32	26	39	42

HS+G, 38T

	28	42	52
14	52	78	97
16	46	68	85
19	38	57	71
22	33	50	61
26	28	42	52
34	21	32	40

DC, 44T

143

	28	46	50
14	52	85	93
16	46	75	81
19	38	63	68
22	33	54	59
26	28	46	50
34	21	35	38

DC(HS), 42T

	28	48	52
14	52	89	97
16	46	78	85
19	38	66	71
22	33	57	61
26	28	48	52
34	21	37	40

DC(HS), 44T

	30	46	50
14	56	85	93
16	49	75	81
19	41	63	68
22	35	54	59
26	30	46	50
34	23	35	38

DC(HS), 40T

	26	41	52
14	48	76	97
16	42	67	85
19	36	56	71
23	29	46	59
27	25	39	50
32	21	33	42

A+G, 44T

	28	46	50
14	52	85	93
16	46	75	81
19	38	63	68
23	32	52	57
27	27	44	48
32	23	37	41

HS+G, 40T

	30	48	52
14	56	89	97
16	49	78	85
19	41	66	71
23	34	54	59
27	29	46	50
32	24	39	42

HS+G, 40T

	26	36	46
14	48	67	85
16	42	59	75
19	36	49	63
23	29	41	52
28	24	33	43
34	20	28	35

A+G, 40T

	28	38	48
14	52	71	89
17	43	58	73
20	36	49	62
23	32	43	54
26	28	38	48
32	23	31	39

DC(A), 38T

	28	46	50
14	52	85	93
17	43	70	76
20	36	60	65
24	30	50	54
27	27	44	48
34	21	35	38

HS+G, 42T

	30	48	52
14	56	89	97
17	46	73	80
20	39	62	68
24	33	52	56
27	29	46	50
34	23	37	40

HS+G, 42T

	28	38	48
14	52	71	89
17	43	58	73
20	36	49	62
24	30	41	52
28	26	35	45
32	23	31	39

A+G, 38T

	26	38	50
14	48	71	93
17	40	58	76
20	34	49	65
24	28	41	54
28	24	35	46
34	20	29	38

A+G, 44T

	28	40	52
14	52	74	97
17	43	61	80
20	36	52	68
24	30	43	56
28	26	37	48
34	21	31	40

A+G, 44T

	28	45	50
14	52	84	93
17	43	69	76
20	36	59	65
24	30	49	54
28	26	42	46
34	21	34	38

HS+G, 42T

	28	46	50
14	52	85	93
17	43	70	76
20	36	60	65
24	30	50	54
28	26	43	46
34	21	35	38

HS+G, 42T

	30	48	52
14	56	89	97
17	46	73	80
20	39	62	68
24	33	52	56
28	28	45	48
34	23	37	40

HS+G, 42T

I: GEAR-INCH FORMULA

Gear-inch numbers are calculated using the formula

$$G = \frac{F \times D}{R}$$

where

F = the number of teeth on the front sprocket (chainring),
D = the diameter of the rear wheel, *in inches,*
R = the number of teeth on the rear sprocket (cog), and
G = the gear-inch number.

This formula is good for *all* size wheels. With D = 27 it produces the gear-inch chart for 27-inch/700-mm wheels; with D = 26 it produces the gear-inch chart for 26-inch wheels (see Chapter 3). For other size wheels, use this formula to find the gear-inch numbers for your bicycle.

Example

For a bicycle having a 24-inch rear wheel (D = 24), connecting a 40T chainring (F = 40) to a 14T cog (R = 14), produces a gear of

$$G = (40 \times 24)/14 = 68.5,$$

which rounds to 69 gear-inches.

J: FORMULAS RELATING SPEED, CADENCE, AND GEAR-INCHES

G = Gear-inch number
C = Cadence (in revolutions per minute)
S = Speed (in miles per hour)

The relationship between G, C, and S is given by the formula

$$\frac{G \times C}{S} = \frac{1056}{pi} = 336.13524.$$

Rounding to 336 produces the following formulas.

S = (G X C)/336

Using a 100-inch gear (G = 100), with a cadence of 80 rpm (C = 80), produces a speed S = (100 X 80)/336 = 23.8, or approximately 24 miles per hour.

C = (336 X S)/G

To go 24 mph (S = 24) in a 100-inch gear (G = 100), you need to pedal with a cadence C = (336 X 24)/100 = 80.64, or approximately 81 revolutions per minute.

G = (336 X S)/C

To go 24 mph (S = 24), with a cadence of 80 rpm (C = 80), you need to use a gear G = (336 X 24)/80 = 100.8, or approximately 101 inches.

K: CHAIN-SHORTENING TESTS

Removing two links of chain can significantly affect the manner in which your rear derailleur behaves, especially when you attempt to shift into the gears which require large amounts of chain. (These are the gears in the lower right portion of your matrix.) If you are able to shift safely into these gears, you may use the shortened chain. You may also use the shortened chain if you are unable to shift into these gears but no harm is caused to your bicycle in the attempts to do so. But if your rear derailleur bends, breaks, or becomes caught in the cogs when you try to shift into these gears, *you must not use the shortened chain.* Even though you do not intend to use the maximum chain gear because of extreme chain deflection, *you must determine the risk you are taking if you inadvertently attempt its use.* If your rear derailleur cannot handle the shorter chain, *it may cause an accident.*

TEST 1

After removing two links of chain, *with your bicycle on a repair stand,* shift into the gear in the upper right corner of your matrix (largest chainring, smallest cog). Then *slowly, one cog at a time,* shift the chain onto larger cogs with your rear derailleur. (You are shifting down the right column of your matrix.) Look carefully to see how your rear derailleur behaves during these shifts, *especially the last one*, as you try to shift into the maximum chain gear. If you are fortunate, your rear derailleur will make this shift normally. Another possibility is that your rear derailleur will be unable to make the shift, but that no harm will be done. *But if it looks as though the derailleur may be forced into the cogs, become bent, or its cage stretched beyond its frontmost limit, STOP! DO NOT COMPLETE THE SHIFT!*

If it appears that your rear derailleur may become bent, broken, or forced into the cogs, you should replace the links you removed and use the longer chain. *Do not use the shorter chain if there is any possibility of breaking parts and causing an accident.*

EXAMPLE 1

G	24	39	48
13	50	81	100
15	43	70	86
17	38	62	76
19	34	55	68
25	26	42	52
32	20	33	41

To apply Test 1 to Gearing G, with your bicycle on a repair stand, shift into the 100-inch gear. Then slowly, one cog at a time, shift into the 86-, 76-, 68-, 52- and, if possible, 41-inch gear, *watching your rear derailleur carefully as you do so.* If you are able to shift into the 41-inch gear, or are unable to do so but no harm is done in the attempt, you may apply Test 2. If it appears that your rear derailleur may bend, break, or be forced into the cogs, you should not use the short-chain method.

If your rear derailleur appears to behave safely during Test 1, you *must* apply Test 2 before deciding that it is safe to use the shorter chain.

TEST 2

In this test you will use your *front* derailleur and attempt to shift into the gears which use the largest amounts of chain. If your middle chainring is significantly smaller than your largest chainring (such as the 24-39-48T chainrings of Gearing G), only the maximum chain gear will be a potential problem. But if your middle and outer chainrings are of nearly equal size (such as 24-44-48T), both the maximum chain gear and the one to its immediate left in your matrix may cause difficulty. If your front derailleur is able to shift the chain into these gears, it may force your *rear* derailleur into the cogs, or to become bent or broken. Consequently you will need to watch your *rear* derailleur carefully as you make this test.

With your bicycle on a repair stand, shift into the gear in the lower left corner of your matrix (smallest chainring, largest cog). If possible, shift the chain to the middle chainring and then, if possible, to the largest chainring (you are shifting across the bottom row of your matrix). It may happen that your front derailleur is unable to complete one of these shifts, but causes no harm to your rear derailleur in the attempt. But if it appears that the front derailleur will be able to shift the chain onto either of the two larger chainrings, *watch your rear derailleur carefully . If the rear derailleur looks as though it may become bent, broken, or forced into the cogs, do not complete the shift!* If it appears that your rear derailleur cannot safely cope with these front derailleur shifts, do not use the shorter chain — the risk of having an accident is too great!

EXAMPLE 2

G	24	39	48
13	50	81	100
15	43	70	86
17	38	62	76
19	34	55	68
25	26	42	52
32	20	33	41

To apply Test 2 to Gearing G, with your bicycle still on a repair stand, begin in the 20-inch gear. Slowly try to shift into the 33- and 41-inch gears (front derailleur), and *watch your rear derailleur as you do so.* If your rear derailleur looks as though it may become bent, broken, or forced into the cogs, do not complete the shift, and do not use the short-chain method. If you are able to shift into the 41-inch gear, or if you are unable to do so but no harm is caused to your bicycle in the attempt, your bicycle has "passed" Test 2.

TEST 3

Test 3 is to *repeat Tests 1 and Test 2 while actually riding your bicycle in a safe location.* Derailleurs can behave differently under the stresses of actual riding than under the no-load conditions of repair stands, and you want to be *certain* that your gearing/derailleur/ chain combination is safe to use.

You may consider using the shorter chain if (1) you are able to shift safely into the maximum chain gear, or (2) you are *unable* to shift into the maximum chain gear with *both* your front and rear derailleurs, but no harm is caused during an attempt to do so. Your derailleurs, being unable to complete this shift, prevent you from shifting into a potentially dangerous gear; and in the process warn you that you are attempting to make an inappropriate shift.

If you are at all tempted to use an unsafe chain arrangement, consider that when you are at home thinking about gearings, it is easy to believe that you will not attempt to shift into a dangerous gear. But when you are actually riding, *you do not always think consciously about your shifting.* It is easy to make incorrect shifts when you are fatigued, talking with other riders, or thinking about your route or other matters. *Do not use the shorter chain if there is any possibility that it may be unsafe.*

L: BLANK GEAR-INCH MATRIX FORMS

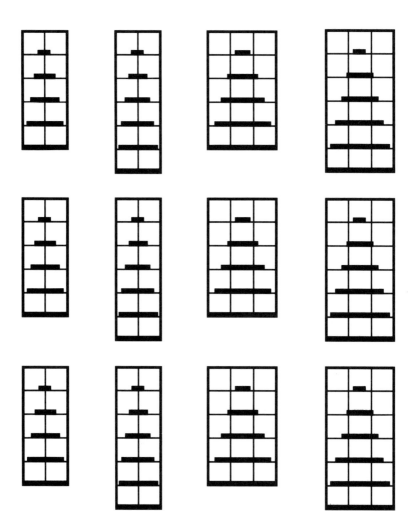

This page may be reproduced for individual use by the purchaser of this book.

FURTHER READING

Allen, John S. *The Complete Book of Bicycle Commuting.* Emmaus, Pa.: Rodale Press, 1981

"Bar-End Clicking." *Bicycling,* April 1988

Barlow, Hank. "Update On Downshifting." *Mountain Bike,* June 1988

Barnett, John. "How Indexed Shifters Work." *Cyclist,* March 1987

_____."How To Adjust Indexed Shifters." *Cyclist,* March 1987

Berto, Frank. "Crossover Gearing." *Bicycling,* July 1988

_____."Front Derailleurs For Racing And Sport Touring." *Bicycling,* February 1986

_____. "Front Derailleurs For Touring And Off Road." *Bicycling,* April 1986

_____."Gear Freaks..." *Bicycling,* July 1988

_____."Gearing To Suit You." *Bicycling,* March 1981

_____."Gearing Up For Loaded Touring." *Bicycling,* July 1984

_____."Latest Word In Triple Cranksets For Touring, The." *Bicycling,* May 1983

_____."Rear Derailleurs For Touring." *Bicycling,* May 1984

_____.*Upgrading Your Bike.* Emmaus, Pa.: Rodale Press, 1988

Bicycling Magazine. *The Bicycle Users' Manual.* Emmaus, Pa.: Rodale Press, 1982

Burne, John. "Gearing By Computer." *Bike Tech,* August 1988

"Click-Shifting For The Masses." *Cyclist,* March 1987

Coles, Charles W., Glenn, Harold T., and Allen, John S. *Glenn's New Complete Bicycle Manual.* New York: Crown Publishers, Inc., 1987

Costantino, Ted. "Suntour's Groupthink Strategy." *Bicycle Guide,* December 1988

Cuerdon, Don. "Gear System Tune-Up." *Bicycling,* June 1988

Forester, John. *Effective Cycling.* Cambridge, Mass.: The MIT Press, 1984

Gaston, Eugene A., M.D. "Preventing Bikers Knees." *Bicycling,* July 1979

"Gearing: A Beginner's Guide." *Mountain Biking,* October 1988

Hammaker, Alan. "Perspectives On Gearing." *Bicycling,* May 1984

Jow, Richard. "The Campagnolo Syncro Shifter." *Bike Tech,* April 1988

Morin, Gregg. "Upgrading To Indexed Shifting." *Mountain Bike,* December 1988

"Mountain Tamer Quad." *Mountain Biking,* November 1988

Okajima, Shinpei. "When Everything Clicks — Evaluating Index System Derailleur Performance." *Bike Tech,* June 1988

Redcay, Jim. "Alpine Gears." *Bicycling,* May 1986

_____."Big Freewheels." *Bicycling,* June 1986

_____."Front Derailleur Adjustment." *Bicycling,* January 1986

Rogers, Thurlow and Roy, Karen E. "Faster Cadence Means Faster Riding." *Cyclist,* February 1987

Roosa, Doug. "Shimano Biopace." *Bicycle Guide,* October 1988

Roosa, Doug and Mills, Keith. "Shimano's Ultimate One-Upsmanship." *Bicycle Guide,* December 1988

Schubert, John. "12 Speeds, What Do They Really Offer Over Ten?" *Bicycling,* April 1983

Weaver, Susan. "Don't Wait Till Your Knees Hurt." *Bicycling,* July 1979

INDEX

About the author:

Dick Marr is an experienced bicycle commuter, recreational rider, and long-distance cycle tourist. His most recent two-wheeled journey took him from the Florida Everglades to British Columbia in Canada, a distance of 5,000 miles as the pedals fly. He's a member of the League of American Wheelmen and BikeCentennial, and three local bicycle clubs near his home in Wheeling, Illinois. Marr teaches high school mathematics in Wheeling, and has written several textbooks in his field. This is his first book for the bicyclist.